Coral and Pearls

He is God!

O peerless Lord! In Thine almighty wisdom Thou hast enjoined marriage upon the peoples, that the generations of men may succeed one another in this contingent world, and that ever, so long as the world shall last, they may busy themselves at the Threshold of Thy oneness with servitude and worship, with salutation, adoration and praise. 'I have not created spirits and men, but that they should worship me.' Wherefore, wed Thou in the heaven of Thy mercy these two birds of the nest of Thy love, and make them the means of attracting perpetual grace; that from the union of these two seas of love a wave of tenderness may surge and cast the pearls of pure and goodly issue on the shore of life. 'He hath let loose the two seas, that they meet each other: Between them is a barrier which they overpass not. Which then of the bounties of your Lord will ye deny? From each He bringeth up greater and lesser pearls.'

O Thou kind Lord! Make Thou this marriage to bring forth coral and pearls. Thou art verily the All-Powerful, the Most Great, the Ever-Forgiving.

'Abdu'l-Bahá

Coral and Pearls

Some Thoughts on the Art of Marriage

by

Mehri Sefidvash

George Ronald
Oxford

George Ronald, Publisher
46 High Street, Kidlington, Oxford OX5 2DN

© Mehri Sefidvash 1998
All Rights Reserved

A Cataloguing-in-Publication entry
is available from the British Library

ISBN 0-85398-422-0

Contents

Preface

When I was a little girl, like all children I had my secret desires, projects and dreams. People used to ask me, 'What do you want to do when you grow up?' Instead of answering, 'I want to be a fireman, a pilot, a teacher or a singer', I was tempted to answer, 'I want to be a writer or a pianist.' But I thought it wiser never to reveal my true ambitions to anyone.

After I had been working with couples as a therapist for a few years, some friends suggested that I describe my experiences in a book. Although I had lectured dozens of times, I told them I wouldn't even think about it! They continued to encourage me and eventually I began to take their suggestions seriously. Finally I said to myself, 'Why not?' So here I am, pen in hand. Perhaps my friends were joking but I prefer to think that they were not. In any case, they reawakened my secret dream of long ago.

The result is neither a text book nor a novel. Indeed, it is difficult to fit it into any category. It is a simple collection of thoughts and feelings based on my experiences and enriched here and there by quotations from the holy scriptures and from well-known writers. It is offered as merely one of a number of helps available to those who wish to understand and enhance their relationship with their partner.

It has been said, 'If you have no courage, no one can give it to you.'[1] I don't agree. With a bit of effort, we can all do what we really want to do. If we want our dreams to come true, it is not enough just to hope. Rather, we must work together, doing everything we can to turn our dreams into reality. This book is just one example of that process at work.

Mehri Sefidvash
Milan, 1997

Acknowledgements

I dedicate this book to all the couples who have, over the years, put their trust in me and opened their hearts. Their courage has helped me understand many aspects of life and has taught me much. I thank them for having shared with me something of their intimacy and their souls.

I wish to thank those friends who gave me the idea to write this book.

I also thank my friend Lelle who has worked, laughed and cried with me down the years. Thanks go to my husband who has given me support, encouragement, stimulation, love and protection during our 24 years of married life – he has shared my anxieties, fears and doubts and has always given me much serenity and joy. Thanks also to my children, Nabil and Noemi, for having supported a mother who probably seemed to them to be a bit strange and rather different from other mothers. Without them my life would lack much of its zest. They are – and always will be – my personal battery chargers.

I am grateful to the National Spiritual Assembly of the Bahá'ís of the United States and the American Baha'i Publishing Trust for their kind permission to reprint the passage in chapter 18 from their publication *A Fortress for Well-Being: Bahá'í Teachings on Marriage*.

Never Take a Relationship for Granted

Are you the one who used
to lose nights of sleep
to come to me?

Marco had to take Bianca to the station in Milan to catch a train to Venice. Deep down, however, they didn't want to part. They spent so much time in idle conversation and in exchanging what should have been one last look that they arrived late and Bianca missed her train, to the great – but secret and unexpressed – joy of both. Marco suggested he drive her as far as Brescia where she could catch the same train. They could thus be together a little longer.

Strangely, they arrived late in Brescia and in Verona, further down the line. By the time they caught up with the train, they had reached Venice and it was midnight. Marco returned home to Milan alone, very tired and sleepy but also very happy and contented. Instead of travelling just a couple of miles, he had travelled nearly four hundred but he had never been so happy. Inwardly he wished the journey would never end. He was completely oblivious to everything else.

Is there anything a person wouldn't do to win the love of someone he or she cares for? What wouldn't we give to see the face of our loved one in a crowd? Nothing is more important and no price is too high, for 'when the fire of love is ablaze, it burneth to ashes the harvest of reason'.[1] When we are in love, achieving our objective is our only reason for living – and the objective is to bring together two individuals with the promise that they will share their futures and live the rest of their lives together.

Why does it sometimes happen that, after we have achieved our objective, we consider it a point of arrival rather than a starting point? When we marry, we often behave as though everything should be taken for granted once the long-awaited and important 'Yes' has been pro-nounced. We seem to be on the right train but are like solitary travellers, each reading our own newspaper. Now and then we cast a glance, perhaps rather sadly, through the window at the countryside through which we are passing and recall all the opportunities we have lost, longing for the green fields we have left behind.

When we are engaged, we tend to be very active. We look after ourselves and take care of our physical appear-ance. We make sure we always appear before our partner in the best possible way. We watch what we say and control our actions. We try to make up quarrels before parting so that no unpleasantness remains. It is easy for us to apologize to one another and make our peace. We each court the other and think that he or she is the most important thing in our lives. We live for the moment when we can see each other, embrace, speak and just be together. Even the smallest things done or experienced together are magical, acquire special meanings and evoke particular emotions such that a simple walk becomes a magnificent adventure. Afterwards we recall all the details and secretly relive every moment.

For a long time, everything remains engraved in our memory. Even after many years have passed, a song can take us back to a particular moment, a moment which, perhaps, in itself was nothing out of the ordinary but which

2

nevertheless was extraordinary for us for the simple reason that all our emotions and senses were concentrated on it. The smells, the noises, the sights of things or certain places can take on special meaning. It is amazing how much attention we pay and how actively we participate in what is going on when we are in the company of the person we love!

I am not suggesting that when we marry we can continue to dedicate the same level of attention to each other as the years go by but we can at least make an effort not to take our relationships for granted and not to fall into the dullness of habit. It is important to make this effort so that our partner can be again for us a truly special person, not 'just' a husband or a wife, the father or the mother of our children, but the person with whom we wish to share our significant moments. We should consciously reaffirm the choice we made at the beginning of the relationship and not simply take it for granted or put up with it because at this point we have to make do.

Kahlil Gibran said that love which is not renewed every day becomes a habit and then a form of slavery. We should, however, distinguish this need to reaffirm our choice from romanticism, which is an attitude more suited to adolescents. It is said that people who need romance are more in love with the idea of love than with a real person. They dream of a storybook life, as their own lives, often lacking strong emotions and drama, seem dull. Such people may even start quarrels in their families to experience more intense feelings – a very childish way to fulfil their needs.

Love should be renewed every day, in the same way that we must continually take care of our homes. We expend much effort on improving our home's decoration, enhancing its beauty and harmony with plants and fresh flowers and, now and again, giving it a fresh coat of paint. This reflects our ongoing effort to make our home environment pleasant, welcoming and warm. A relationship that is not renewed can become like a house that was decorated many years ago but now has cracks in the walls, chips in the furniture and a pathetic layer of dust on the silk flowers that once looked so good.

Regular Servicing

*The battery is flat
just when I need the car.*

Ellen went through periodic crises when she would question her otherwise apparently serene relationship with her husband. When she was in a crisis she would raise such subjects as the lack of true communication between her and her husband or their different ideas about bringing up the children.

Her husband, Frank, usually put these crises down to female 'problems' – pre-menstrual tension, pregnancy, breast-feeding – or to stress caused by overwork. He never took Ellen's criticisms of their relationship seriously. Indeed, he saw them not so much as criticisms but as symptoms of Ellen's malaise and discontent. It was easier for him to attribute any problems to causes outside the relationship, or to his wife alone, rather than to the relationship itself. Personally, he didn't have any problems and he was quite content as things stood.

Frank was so blind to the situation, or so superficial, that he was dumbfounded when Ellen finally decided to leave him. He couldn't understand why. He was deeply upset. He gradually realized that he should have listened with more attention to Ellen but by that time she had already lost her confidence in him and had developed a dislike for everything he stood for. She had lost the will to continue the struggle and was bitter and offended.

When a relationship ends, it is always the fault of both partners. It is probably true that Ellen nagged. Perhaps she was incapable of being firm on matters of principle and more flexible on secondary issues – she did tend to put everything on the same level. Frank, in the confusion, certainly underestimated the seriousness of the situation. Like many men, he had been his mother's pet and for many years his wife had accepted and put up with this; but finally she tired and decided to make a complete break with everything, including her husband.

It is difficult for us to forget to service our car – experience teaches us that if we do, it usually breaks down. When we buy a house, it is equally difficult to neglect it, to leave it as it is for many years without touching up the paint on the walls and the woodwork, replacing broken panes of glass or repairing leaky pipes. Not even a pair of shoes remains exactly as it was when we first saw it in the shop window – shoes require a brush and a polish to keep them serviceable. In all sorts of situations, we naturally, spontaneously and logically check things out and see whether they need attention.

Strangely, our marriage, which is perhaps the most important thing in our lives, is often the only thing we believe does not need servicing or redecorating. We take it for granted that the foundations on which the marriage was built will last forever.

It is important to understand that love does not die 'just like that'. It dies through negligence, lack of care and forgetfulness. It dies because of ignorance, indifference or blindness. It dies because we take it for granted. These are much more serious than any mistakes we might make in the marriage. Often it is not that love itself dies; it is simply that we no longer put any life into our relationship.

We know that for a seed to grow it needs water, light and the right soil. If we want a plant to give us delicious and healthy fruit, we know it needs continuous care and attention and, when necessary, pruning. We should realize that a relationship is also a living organism and must therefore continue to grow, as, otherwise, it will wither and die.

In some cases, one of the marriage partners is very surprised when the other decides to separate and this is because he or she was unaware of this slow process of withering. As one partner was not prepared for this development, he or she often finds the situation unjust and may accuse the other of not having forewarned him or her. Usually, however, there has been a continuous stream of messages from one spouse which should have made the situation quite clear but these messages were ignored or minimized by the other person, who was, perhaps, unwilling to jeopardize the stability of the relationship by responding to the messages. However, it is precisely because of this unwillingness to face facts that, paradoxically, a relationship ends. Thus many people find themselves in a situation where they have lost their family but don't understand how or why.

Loving someone does not simply involve strong emotions. It is also a commitment and a promise. Sensations and emotions are passing phenomena on which we cannot base a love that is to last for a long time. Loving is basically a commitment to working together for a whole lifetime. As 'Abdu'l-Bahá says:

> . . . marriage is the commitment of the two parties one to the other, and their mutual attachment of mind and heart. Each must, however, exercise the utmost care to become thoroughly acquainted with the character of the other, that the binding covenant between them may be a tie that will endure forever. Their purpose must be this: to become loving companions and comrades and at one with each other for time and eternity . . .[1]

Someone once said, 'Getting together is a beginning, staying together is progress and working together is success.' We must find the time to live our life as a couple and, consequently, find time for our love. Otherwise, we are just living in the same place. If we become introverted or stop trying to make the relationship work, the relationship will, like a boat, drift aimlessly or end up in trouble when the water becomes rough.

Communication plays a vital role in the process of keeping a relationship alive. It is very important to speak and to express sentiments in words. We cannot simply rely on symbolic gestures, take things for granted or expect our partner to 'understand' that we love him or her. Love needs to be heard as well as felt.

Active listening helps us to grow. As we go through our lives – as we evolve – many things we have learned in the past may have to be abandoned and relearned. True growth, the most visible sign of our maturity, is change. If we do not want to change, if we do not see the point of it, and our positions and attitudes remain static, fossilized and rigid, we have a very small chance of keeping our relationship alive for long.

When two people decide to marry, each brings to the relationship a different set of experiences, opinions and habits. These are often incompatible. If we want a relationship to last, we must accept minor compromises and be flexible, whether we like it or not. The most important thing is to be firm where fundamental principles are involved and more flexible in the secondary aspects of life. Strangely, at times, we do exactly the opposite and take a very rigid stand on small things, in this way making the other's life a misery.

We often hear people – including ourselves – say, 'That's the way I am', 'I just can't' and 'I'm too old to change'. When we say such things we run the great risk of believing what we say, thus limiting our options. If we do not give ourselves the opportunity, or even the hope, to do things differently or to do new things, love itself can become a cage in which we feel ourselves trapped. If we insist on believing that there are no alternatives or continue to blame other people for our problems, considering them responsible for our lack of satisfaction with our own situation, we will always see ourselves as victims without hope.

As time passes, marriage partners often begin to neglect one another and their relationship becomes a monotony of gestures and words that were once full of meaning and enthusiasm but have become purely conventional. In a relationship, few things are more harmful than predictability and boredom. If we are not careful, our lives will fall into an insidious and deadly routine which, like a cobweb that grows undisturbed, enveloping everything, is noticed only when it has covered most of our lives. Fortunately, it is possible, if we wish to do so, to overcome apathy with a bit of enthusiasm or by doing something surprising and unexpected, by letting our imaginations run riot and suggesting a project or activity that is out of the ordinary.

If we have the feeling that our sentiments are dulling, what we really need to do, now and then, is something amusing and different: take an unplanned little trip, give an unexpected gift or just do something crazy.

This reminds me of a story a friend once told me:

> In the first few years of our marriage, we had very serious financial problems. Despite this, when our child was born I decided to draw all of my savings out of the bank to buy a watch that my wife told me she liked very much. She was very pleased but also very surprised, as our future was so uncertain. We have never forgotten the pleasure which that crazy gesture gave us. Through all the years, even after we achieved economic well-being, no other gift has ever had the same effect and the same meaning for us.

Another couple, of course, might consider this the height of irresponsibility, but these two saw in this spontaneous action an act of love which drew them closer together.

If we analyze the relationships of friends or acquaintances that have ended badly, we will realize that marriages fail only rarely because of important matters or events. Usually, these relationships have foundered on small things that are apparently insignificant and which, taken singly, are of little or no importance but when taken together in the long run have a devastating effect.

In our marriage relationship, we tend to be passive. Consequently, when difficulties arise, we give up without a fight, as we are convinced that a relationship has a life of its own, completely independent of our will and our efforts to give it new life.

No one has ever said that love is easy, just as life itself is not easy. Love is a continuous search, or a journey with all its obstacles, frustrations, anxieties and doubts. If we are looking for tranquillity, perhaps we should stay single and live a life without the tests and challenges a partner can bring, with only our shadows for company and our own voices to listen to. When a person becomes a part of our life, a certain amount of disturbance – or even disruption – is inevitable.

We learn from science that adaptability is the basis of survival. Those who are unwilling to adapt and change their behaviour or consider compromise a sign of weakness do not understand that there is a world of difference between giving way to another person because we are forced to do so, or because we are threatened, and giving way because we want to, or out of affection. Indeed, such flexibility, far from being a weakness, is a sign of great strength of mind. Between people who love each other, giving is very important. What we think we are losing in power, control or self-affirmation, we are in fact recovering in maturity, wisdom and serenity.

Obviously, we cannot always love a person for a long time in the same way, at every moment. It isn't possible and we shouldn't expect to do so. As Anne Linderbergh remarked, there is not just one harvest for the heart – the seed of love must continually be replanted.

The couple in the film *The War of the Roses* began married life in an atmosphere of harmony and promise but over the years, for various reasons, they became increasingly estranged until the situation degenerated into a real war with no quarter given. They showed no pity for one another and continued to struggle until both died. What struck me most about this film was the last scene. A lawyer, a specialist in divorce (and the narrator of the story), tells the man who has come to him for advice, 'And now go away and try to remember just one of the reasons why you fell in love with your wife, and start again from there.'

It is incredible how two people who are able to join forces to overcome serious crises or trials are unable to settle minor quarrels which they then allow to grow and get out of hand. It is useful, from time to time, to clear up any minor misunderstandings by discussing them openly, before a molehill becomes a mountain. 'Abdu'l-Bahá advises:

> When differences present themselves, take counsel together in secret, lest others magnify a speck into a mountain. Harbour not in your hearts any grievance, but rather explain its nature to each other with such frankness and understanding that it will disappear, leaving no remembrance.[2]

By clearing away the clouds, both see the sun again and receive its light and heat.

Nearly all of us have had the experience of a situation in which there was a lot of tension or people's nerves were frayed and a shared laugh was enough to make the atmosphere warm and joyful again. All too often we underestimate the importance of a smile, an embrace, a kind word, a sincere compliment or the giving of one's attention. It is precisely the small things that can change difficult moments into special ones.

Most of us are not used to embracing others, even those we love. Embraces are often only given in a sexual context or on those very rare occasions when something serious has happened, such as a bereavement. Of course, the need for physical warmth does become stronger in dramatic circumstances. We don't think it necessary, however, to hug one another in the course of our daily life.

Scientific research has demonstrated that tears shed in moments of great emotion contain a chemical substance, produced by the central nervous system, which eliminates pain. It is therefore useful, or rather necessary, to cry when we are in pain. Hugging too can help us overcome depression, as it helps the body's immune system to regain its tone and vitality and helps relieve tension and tiredness and even some kinds of pain, such as headache, stiff neck and backache.

In a marriage, embracing one another every day helps to strengthen ties and greatly decreases tensions. It has been found that when a person is touched by another the quantity of haemoglobin in his blood increases. This substance is one of the components of blood that supplies vital reserves of oxygen to all the organs of the body, including the heart and the brain. An increase in the amount of haemoglobin therefore tones the whole body and helps prevent certain diseases. It also helps healing. It has been said that 'Getting into the habit of embracing your husband or your wife, your children, your relatives and your friends is a wonderful way to improve the quality of life.'

Consider. How long has it been since you last looked lovingly into the eyes of your partner? How long ago did you stop exchanging tender glances? Do you still notice the slight changes in the colour of your spouse's eyes?

Someone once said, 'What hurts me is not losing you but the regret that I was unable to really meet you at the thousand turning-points of our lives.' Let this not be our refrain.

3

Love Affairs

*The grass is always greener
on the other side of the fence.*

Glenda is very impetuous. Everything she does, she does
with gusto. You can't help noticing her, especially physically.
Her husband, Stephen, is one of those men who would like
to remain young forever. He just can't stand the idea that the
years are passing for him as for everyone else. He was repeat-
edly unfaithful to his wife but more for devilment and
because he is shallow than because he was convinced of
what he was doing. Glenda insists on having everything
under her control so when she realized what Stephen was up
to, she simply left him. Neither his tears nor his acting the
abandoned child could persuade her to change her decision.

It is obvious that the intrusion of a third party into a
couple's relationship can trigger a crisis. It is exactly like
what happens when a virus attacks the body, causing illness
and suffering. When we have a viral attack, we consult the
best doctors and do all we can to treat the illness with medi-
cines. Sometimes the illness lasts a long time and is followed
by a difficult period of convalescence. Other times we may
need an operation that leaves us with a scar for the rest of
our lives. We may be more susceptible to certain illnesses

because we are run down or there is not enough of a particular antibody in our system. However, we now know how to prevent certain illnesses and are beginning to realize that prevention is a more effective strategy than cure in providing good health. Should we fall ill, we are more likely to recover if we have kept ourselves generally healthy than if our systems were not quite right in the first place.

Marriages may also show signs of illness. For example, a man may be more susceptible to the temptation to have an affair when he is going through an identity crisis. Typically, a man goes through this critical period when he is in his forties. He feels he needs to reestablish his identity and rediscover his true image, which he believes he has lost. During this time it is difficult for him to understand that the passage of time has given him greater experience, wisdom, maturity and, often, more charisma and has not just taken away his youth, enthusiasm and energy.

If a man has these doubts of an existential or physical nature, he will seek opportunities to assert his identity, to reassure himself and to obtain gratification outside himself or outside the marriage. For him, the ability to attract another woman is the best guarantee, from all points of view, that time has done him no irreparable harm.

The problem is identical for a woman. She may be tired of her daily routine, which gives her security but is also very boring. She may believe that her life is empty, without excitement and romance.

Women are often very romantic and think in romantic terms and their daydreams may be very different from their daily lives. A woman's husband may seem never to change his response to her – her more or less explicit messages inviting him to speak to her, to show affection or simply to be nice to her may at best receive the stock answer, 'I married you, so I must love you. I don't drink or smoke and I'm not unfaithful to you. I work more for you than for myself, to make sure you have a comfortable life and ensure the future of you and our children is secure. I don't know what else you want from me. Why are you never satisfied?'

In such cases, it may happen that a woman will find another man more attractive. He may not give her all the essential things her husband does and may not offer the security of a future life together but he does give her some of his time, makes her feel she is still desirable and perhaps attends to all those things that her husband often neglects.

The situations described here may seem trite but they are typical and very common. Of course, many of us will not recognize ourselves in these scenarios but they are simply examples and many variants may occur in real life. It is possible, however, to pass through such a phase unscathed.

We often take for granted the attentions of our own partner but feel very gratified or flattered by the attentions of another person. We are pleased when someone appreciates us and few of us would deny that we have secretly smiled at the thought of being admired for our body or mind. This is all quite natural and is a legitimate gift we receive from outside our marriage. It becomes a problem only if we dedicate our energies to searching for such flattery and become obsessed with looking for gratification of our egos because we feel unable to find within ourselves strength, energy and positive qualities. If we reach the point when we are prepared to make sacrifices just to receive such attention, when we are incapable of making gifts to ourselves or to recognize those we receive from our companion, or when these gifts from others are not enough, when our life depends solely on the positive image others have of us, then we are living to build our image rather than to *be*.

It has never been so true as it is today that appearance counts more than reality. Image has become, for many of us, more important than being. Today we are in a sort of vacuum in the sense that we have rejected the models, ideals and standards of the past but have not yet developed new ones. We therefore make do and accept the standards which the mass media and our wholly materialistic society offer. One of the most common images is the young female body, with all its positive implications of youth and sexual attractiveness. The same applies to the young male body, of course. These images – to be slim, beautiful, young, rich and successful – are widely promoted as the ideal. The myth of beauty and youth at all costs is more sought after today than it has ever been. Through exercise and diets, weight-lifting and face-packs, we try to imitate to the best of our ability the models and images that are dominant in modern society. Even our clothes are determined by such images – fashion, with its continuous and sudden changes, forcing us to adapt if we want to look 'right'. The important thing is that the clothes cost a lot or that the designer's name is well-known. In real life, however, no one but the truly rich can ever feel really comfortable with their clothes.

The women we see on television – the most influential information medium – especially in advertisements, are always carefree, smiling and affectionate, even when the floor has just been dirtied by the family dog coming in from the beautiful garden with its perfectly kept lawn. Women in advertisements keep smiling even when their babies make enormous stains on their best clothes or upset a table laid for dinner – they always have exactly the right product to hand to fix everything, so they do not need to become upset. The housewife lightheartedly polishes the floor wearing high-heel shoes and a silk blouse. Any man watching this on TV naturally makes a comparison with his own wife sitting next to him on the sofa and sees that she has none of the beauty or good humour of the woman on the screen. The result of any such comparison, conscious or unconscious, is a foregone conclusion.

A man may wonder why his wife does not become wildly passionate after just one glance or kiss, as happens in films, and why she is so difficult about the 'preliminaries'. A woman may wonder why it is only her husband who doesn't have a magnetic gaze and why he doesn't lavish her with caresses. She wonders why he doesn't walk miles in the pouring rain to buy her chocolates or, better still, perfume and diamonds, perhaps stealing a flower on the way back just for her. Why is he always asking for something if a real man never has to ask for anything? She looks sadly at the man dozing off at her side and sighs for the prince charming on his white horse who somehow got lost in the forest. Perhaps one day she'll meet him, although he may look like that nice grocer in the little shop over the way.

So important is our image to us that we may fall into the trap of idolizing another person because he or she admires us. Similarly, it is often that person's image that we idolize and not the person himself. In either case, we are bound to be disappointed for the other person can never live up to our expectations completely.

We are often told that in matters of love we should follow our instincts. This implies that we are free to abandon any moral considerations, that we are able to ignore our moral conditioning and training and that we can act in complete freedom. However, if we think about it, we will realize that not even animals are free, as instinct itself is a form of biological and natural conditioning from which they cannot escape. The same applies to humans. Allowing ourselves to be governed by our hormones or instincts is not freedom. True freedom involves, among other things, deciding of our own free will to follow certain moral and ethical rules and principles.

We may sometimes think that there is no further reason to remain with our partner, that finding a new partner will make us happy. We often forget that wherever we go we take ourselves with us. There is no way out. We can change the scenery, move to a new house, change our partner and our friends, completely transform the external situation – and for a time things may seem better – but in the end we are still ourselves and have to face the consequences of our same behaviours, attitudes, emotions and reactions.

When we find a new partner, for some time we may feel quite satisfied. We forget that we bring with us into this new relationship all our weaknesses, limitations, fears and problems. Because we have not changed, the new relationship resurrects the problems of the old. We are back to square one: we are still unhappy, we still have the same anxieties and are bothered by the same things. If we truly want a deep and long-lasting relationship, if we truly want to find love, there is only one way we can achieve this. We must change inside. There is no other way.

If it is we who have to change inside, perhaps we should seriously consider, before we decide to leave our partners for someone else, whether this will indeed solve our difficulties. There may be many reasons why we should stay together.

4

Openness and Frankness

The best way to tell the
truth is to say it with love.

In a marriage, as in life, it is important to know oneself and one's own potential and internal motivations. Bahá'u'lláh reminds us that 'the station conferred' upon our 'own inmost being' is 'the station of the knowledge' of our own 'selves'.[1] Erich Fromm said that love is an art, just as living is an art. If we want to know how to love, we should do the same as we would if we wanted to learn music, painting, medicine or engineering. To learn the art of love we must first know ourselves well. This doesn't mean that we'll never make any mistakes but that we'll realize, in good time and with humility, that we have in fact made a mistake. It is essential to remember always that our greatest strength lies in service to others and in our willingness to help. In a stone building, the strongest material is used for the foundations. It has been said that up to now our society has used people and loved things; now we should love people and use things. If we could apply this in our everyday lives, we would achieve a better quality of life both for ourselves and for others.

As well as knowing ourselves, in preparing for marriage, it is vitally important to know the character of the person we intend to marry too. 'Abdu'l-Bahá says: 'Each must . . . exercise the utmost care to become thoroughly acquainted with the character of the other, that the binding covenant between them may be a tie that will endure forever.'[2] Unfortunately, in many cases, habit and the conventional approach to courtship prevent us from knowing our future partner well. The circumstances in which most couples meet – at leisure-time activities, work, parties, etc. – are not always the best occasions for evaluating a person's character. In fact, for many people, the whole aim of courtship is to hide their real selves. It is therefore not surprising that people who marry after this kind of courtship are disappointed when they begin to experience together the realities of family life and bringing up children. Exploring another's character, as well as our own, requires patience, tact and wisdom and a commitment to openness – the very qualities needed in the marriage itself.

'The bond that united hearts most perfectly', 'Abdu'l-Bahá told a prospective bridegroom, 'is loyalty.'[3] Loyalty in a relationship is based on trust and respect, on a mutual and voluntary pact. As the relationship is constantly evolving, this pact must also evolve. Trust and respect are built on openness and honesty.

We sometimes hear a person say, 'My only good point is my frankness. I don't mince words and I say exactly what's on my mind. I'm not a hypocrite. I always tell people what I think to their faces . . .'

Nobody would condemn a person who said this. On the contrary, he or she would be praised as an example of transparency. But how many of us are frank because we want to be transparent and honest and how many are frank because, consciously or unconsciously, we intend to hurt or offend someone or get our own back on them? How many of us are frank because we feel ourselves superior to another or, simply, because we want to get something off our mind and burden someone else with it. The difficulty with frankness is that its use can appear to be quite legitimate and it is universally considered meritorious whereas sometimes it is used as a way of hurting another person or gaining ascendancy over him.

It is said that 'the tongue is mightier than the sword'. Bahá'u'lláh describes the tongue as a 'smouldering fire'.[4] This weapon requires no licence, is always with us and can generally be used with impunity. Who knows how many people we have hurt during our lives with this weapon without ever realizing what we have done.

I don't want to encourage hypocrisy or the resort to devious diplomacy but I do want to urge people not to abuse frankness or to use it indiscriminately, without first considering whether their intentions are pure and what the object is that they want to achieve.

Generally speaking, those who hurt others, or at least tend to express their own negative feelings often, are people who suffer a lot. There may be many causes for this suffering arising out of widely differing circumstances, including particular events in a person's life or those disappointments that are inevitable for everyone. We all know that a wounded animal is dangerous because, in its suffering, it becomes fierce and attacks even when it is not necessary to do so for its safety or self-preservation. Its victims may be innocent passersby or even those who try to help. The same applies to humans. A person who is suffering can become very wicked and hurtful and this can be manifested either directly or indirectly. Sometimes indirect wickedness or hurtfulness is disguised as open-mindedness and frankness.

Sometimes we behave negatively towards our partner, or even ourselves, out of negligence or superficiality rather than wickedness or an intention to hurt. We act like a child who, for lack of attention or through clumsiness, damages precious things because he simply doesn't know what they are worth and cannot or will not control his actions. Only when the child realizes the value of an object, which may be rare or irreplaceable, and can control his actions will such damage cease. Maturity is accompanied by greater awareness and greater responsibility. Blaming and punishing or creating a sense of guilt serves no useful purpose.

The more we become aware of the value and preciousness of certain aspects of life – the more we truly come to know ourselves – the more attention we pay to them. For example, the more we understand the positive influence that purity and honesty have on our inner development the more we make efforts to preserve our integrity. Otherwise, there is no reason why, in a world of thieves, we should be the only honest person around.

By knowing ourselves, by being open and honest with ourselves, we can discover the character of others and can learn to be open and honest with them.

5

Respect

*Don't make your partner pay
too dearly for the love you give.*

Silvia thought, 'I love Luke but I don't like him.' She was convinced, though, that if she married him, through the power of her love and with a little persuasion, she could change him. However, as always happens in such cases, her disappointment and frustration were proportional to her hope and belief that she could change another person. Even the Divine Teachers find it difficult to change people, and, when they do succeed, such transformations are called miracles.

Because she is continuously using all of her energy to change Luke, Silvia increasingly feels emotionally drained, disappointed and, above all, angry. She finds it hard to focus her attention on herself and thus cannot understand why she feels this need to control another person. Luke, apparently, leaves her to it, as if he were merely looking on, watching something that really has nothing to do with him. At times, he acts the victim but in fact he is just a spectator, passively watching the whole scene. Subconsciously he holds to the thought expressed in the Oriental saying: 'Wait on the river bank and, sooner or later, you will see the corpse of your enemy float by.' Neither Silvia nor Luke has respect for the other.

In modern, civilized families, weapons have changed. They are much more sophisticated than in the past, as if they have benefited from the developments of modern technology. But just as peace is not simply a state of non-war, respect doesn't just mean not throwing plates or shouting abuse at one another.

Bahá'u'lláh urges us, 'Deny not My servant should he ask anything from thee, for his face is My face'.[1] Symbolically, then, respect is seeing and loving the image of God in the other person – and the image of God is always positive. We only have to go beyond outward appearances and use our inner vision to discover the mines of precious gems hidden in each of us. If we fail to use this inner vision, or fail to receive true education about life, what we will reveal about ourselves and find in others will be more like worthless rubble than priceless jewels.

A trap we all fall into is to hurt the most those we love the most – we fail to respect them. We continue to correct what we consider to be their mistakes, we criticize their decisions, we try to change their attitudes and we argue about matters of form. Of course, there is nothing wrong in expecting the best from those we love but to try to improve our partner by continually making negative comments about him or criticizing him is certainly not the best way to help him better himself or to show him respect.

The origin of the word 'respect' comes from the Latin *respicere*, that is, to look at or consider a person for what he or she is, to know the person as an individual. Respect means wanting the other person to grow and develop into what he is and can be. Respect automatically excludes exploitation and selfish expectations. To have respect for a person we love means having the desire that he should grow and develop according to his own wishes and his own capabilities, and not just because this is useful for us.

If I love someone, I always feel close to him, whatever choices he may make for his own development. I accept him for what he is and not for what he would be if he were to adapt himself to me. Respect exists only where there is freedom. As has been said, love is the child of liberty. It is clear that respect is possible only if both partners have achieved independence, if they can each stand on their own two feet and live without one having to lean on the other for support. We know that when we begin a love relationship, we must sacrifice a part of ourselves. It is important, however, to ensure that this does not mean that we completely lose our own personalities.

Someone once said that a love relationship is one in which the person I love is free to be himself, to laugh with me but not at me, to cry with me but not because I made him cry. Many of us want our partners to love us in the way we think best and not as they do, so we try to control our relationships. If we deceive ourselves into thinking that through our love we can change our partner or his life, we will become angry, frustrated and disappointed when we realize that we cannot.

Respect also means silence, a precious resource. A moment of reflection can help us find solutions to problems. As 'Abdu'l-Bahá reminds us, 'In that state of [reflection] you put certain questions to your spirit and the spirit answers: the light breaks forth and the reality is revealed.'[2] Creativity and spirituality come to us mainly in our moments of peace and quiet.

In the life of any couple there are moments that are very difficult and it is hard for each partner to show respect for the other. It is precisely at such critical moments that we must show how patient we can be. Overcoming difficulties requires great ability. In exasperating situations, we must find the time to pause and reflect if we are not afterwards to regret our words and actions. The Golden Rule, 'Do unto others what you would have them do unto you' or 'Do not do to others that which you do not wish done to yourself' is a useful guideline for action. By putting ourselves in our partner's shoes now and again, by trying to discover what he or she feels, we can come to realize many things about our partner, we learn to respect him more fully and we open our hearts to new levels of understanding, compassion, tenderness and intimacy. In many circumstances where tension is great and emotions are running high, knowing how to say 'I'm sorry' can reduce tension and make the other person more inclined to recognize his or her own mistakes.

Each of us has many things inside that cause us to suffer: a painful past, unfulfilled dreams, mistakes and hidden hopes. Digging up our partner's past mistakes in a tense moment or using his weak points to humiliate him, to demonstrate we are right, to give ourselves the feeling we are superior or simply to win, can destroy in a minute a relationship that was built up gradually over a long time.

This is one reason why the love we feel for our partner should not depend solely on externalities or spring from only a superficial harmony. Love and respect must be based on more enduring qualities. In this connection it is useful to recall here the saying that a man who falls in love with a woman for her beauty is very different from a man who loves a woman and so can see the beauty in her. It is much more difficult – but much more gratifying – to see a person's inner beauty and character than his outward appearance and personality.

Self-respect

Loving relationships require that each partner respects not only the other person but himself. Respecting ourselves can sometimes be difficult. We may have been told as children that we were bad or lazy or stupid and this thought may have stayed with us. However, if we recognize in ourselves the truth of the words given us by Bahá'u'lláh, 'Veiled in My immemorial being and in the ancient eternity of My essence, I knew My love for thee; therefore I created thee, have engraved on thee Mine image and revealed to thee My beauty',[3] we will accept that we are worthy and have dignity.

Lawrence is 26 and Monica is 24. Both of them have office jobs. When one day I asked Monica to come for an appointment the next evening, she told me that she didn't know whether she would be free. When I asked her why she didn't know what she was going to do the next day, she replied that it all depended on a phone call from her fiance. I asked her if they had made a tentative arrangement to meet but had not yet confirmed it. After a long explanation, I discovered that Monica had a tentative date with Lawrence every day. Whenever he was free and had nothing else to do, he expected her to be ready to go out with him. Monica had even given up going to the gym twice a week in case it clashed with Lawrence's free time – she felt it wouldn't be very nice to disappoint him.

Rather confused by Monica's responses, I asked her whether she didn't consider Lawrence's lack of respect for her personal freedom a bit too much. After all, they were only engaged now. Imagine what it would be like when they were married! Monica, looking even more confused than I, asked me why I couldn't understand that Lawrence felt great love for and attachment to her and that he didn't want to waste even one second of the time he could spend with her. Giving up the gym and other activities was really of no consequence, she said. So, I said to myself after Monica had left, love, at times, is not just blind but also deaf and stupid. I don't know what happened to that couple but just thinking about them makes me shudder.

All the Divine Teachers have told us that human beings are essentially spiritual beings, manifestations of life and, therefore, sacred. An awareness of the sacredness of each individual enables us to feel passionate about events that take place in our world and compassion for the people involved in them. A sound relationship takes into account the unique nature of each partner and the interaction between the two.

Most of us have been educated to compete, excel and conquer but have been taught little about loving ourselves. If we don't love ourselves, how can we love others? It is an old-fashioned idea that loving oneself is egoistic and promotes a feeling of superiority towards others. The more modern understanding, founded on the concept of equality, is that love is based on feelings and is an indispensable source of strength and energy for our growth and development.

Just as we are urged to see the image of God in others, we need to heed the words of Bahá'u'lláh, who, speaking with the voice of God, tells us, 'Turn thy sight unto thyself, that thou mayest find Me standing within thee, mighty, powerful and self-subsisting.'[4] We must have a good opinion of ourselves and be capable of loving ourselves. If I have a good relationship with myself, I am relaxed and happy and so I think positively. I don't have to conquer anyone or steal anything, neither do I have to be at the centre of everyone's attention. I can turn my attention to others and do not have to focus on myself. If, on the other hand, I feel weak, I must look after myself because I am small and need protecting. I focus on myself and spoil myself to the point that my entire being revolves around me. This is how one becomes an egoist. Thus if it is a virtue to love our neighbours, as they are human beings, it must be equally virtuous – and not sinful – to love ourselves. We must not think that God, in creating the masterpiece that is humankind, failed only with us.

The idea 'love thy neighbour as thyself' implies, above all, self-respect, which cannot be separated from the love and understanding of another human being. Having a positive vision of oneself is indispensable for a satisfactory relationship with one's partner; self-esteem is fundamental to a mature relationship.

We may occasionally feel rejected or hurt but if we accept that we have endless resources and an ability to recover, we will find the courage to fight back and have another go at life. When we are feeling depressed, we must appeal to our dignity to help us out of this state. By becoming an actor in our lives and not a spectator of it, we can change the course of our lives whenever we wish and in whatever direction we choose. We often blame others for our unhappiness, suffering and discomfort but if we understand that no one and nothing but ourselves can shape us, then we will take charge of our own selves and free others of responsibility for our situation.

We can probably all recall a teacher who didn't like us and that's why we got bad marks or someone who had been recommended by a bigwig for a job we had applied for and that's why we're unemployed. Perhaps we had a false friend who stole our fiance and that's why we're all alone in the world. Bearing a grudge is self-destructive, as it prevents us from getting on and starting again. We waste our energies in negative actions and this makes us feel emotionally drained, keeps us in a state of mistrust and suspicion, destroys our creativity and delays our growth.

Love makes us see a wrong we have suffered from a different angle, separately from the person who has wronged us. This helps us avoid exaggerated reactions. Love is the main reason we are able to forgive someone. La Rochefoucauld remarked that each of us forgives in proportion to our capacity to love. If you find a person who will love you because of and not despite your differences, you will have someone by your side who will love you forever.

Jealousy

In a loving relationship, feelings of jealousy are common and can occur frequently. We needn't be afraid of feeling jealous. It is a normal and natural emotion. Anyone who is in love feels jealous sooner or later. However, it is very important that we do not allow jealousy to become a corrosive acid that destroys us and those we love, for as 'Abdu'l-Bahá says, 'jealousy, like unto poison, vitiates the very essence of love'.[5] Rather we should see jealousy as a challenge for us to grow in self-respect and in our inner knowledge. The choice is ours.

When jealousy is very pronounced, it, like all extreme feelings, inevitably becomes destructive and prevents us from seeing things clearly. It imprisons us in a vicious circle, gives us no respite and makes us feel impotent. In most cases, extreme jealousy is the product of insecurity and a lack of consideration and respect for oneself or one's partner. When we are very jealous, we begin to lose our rationality and are no longer able to appreciate our strong points and good characteristics. All our weaknesses, limitations and complexes are emphasized until we feel completely inadequate and insignificant.

By losing our sense of dignity and value, we become the cause of our own jealousy. Blaming others for what we feel leads to no positive results. Things will change only when we accept responsibility for our jealousy as an emotion that is harmless unless it makes us act in a negative manner. Removing the burden of this responsibility from others is an important step towards awareness and maturity. We can solve the problem of jealousy by using it as a way to get to know ourselves better and as a positive element in self-education. For example, we can ask ourselves why in this situation our self-esteem is so low and what the real reasons are for our feelings of inadequacy. What do we really need? Who else but ourselves can help us at such times?

We can never and should never want to possess another human being. The decision to come together as a couple and to stay together is a choice made by two independent people who, in a certain sense, will always remain separate.

We need to learn that loving another person means that we want him to be himself. If we are too possessive we may stifle the very thing we want to be vital. Dinah Mullock Craik reminds us that love that demands love in return is a barter and causes only pain whereas love that gives unstintingly receives love in return.

6

Mature Love

*Freedom is simply the opportunity
to better ourselves.*
Albert Camus

Max needed help and so did Melissa. Both of them were
alone in the world and both of them had difficult pasts.
Deep down Max was a dreamer, while Melissa was practical
and down to earth. They thought that by marrying they
would overcome their problems and receive the help they
needed.

In marriage, each partner brings his or her own share of
suffering, solitude, disappointments and unexpressed expectations. Instead of the pain being divided by two, it's
multiplied by two, as the laws of mathematics clearly
demonstrate. How can the sum of two problems give half a
problem? Even a child is able to understand this. However,
when we are in love and impatient to reach a state of com-
pleteness, it becomes difficult to behave according to logic.

Once they were married, Melissa and Max quickly fell
into the habit of concentrating more on the material aspects
of their lives than on developing their relationship, which
was full of the problems both had brought to it. Their material possessions seemed to be the only consistent things in

their lives. After a while, they took a good look at each other and realized that neither of them recognized the other any longer. They felt betrayed and did not realize that, rather than a person, they had in fact each married the image of their own expectations.

Many times when I have listened to couples I have felt that the recriminations, complaints and accusations have arisen because the foundation of the relationship between the partners is weak. Because there is no true bond between them, at times one or the other acts in a way that evokes pity, he or she playing the victim just to force the other to be kind, agreeable and loving. One often tries to occupy the other's personal space, as he is not capable of creating his own space in which he can grow harmoniously with his partner.

To lay a solid and mature foundation for a healthy relationship, it is necessary that each partner know himself or herself and come to know and understand the character of the other. A person who does not know himself often makes decisions that he cannot uphold or makes commitments that he cannot honour. Such a person also finds it difficult to judge other people's characters. A person who does not know himself is not really prepared for engagement or marriage.

In laying a strong foundation for a relationship, each partner must be helped to feel complete within himself or herself. Neither partner must depend too much on the other and both must be able to express fully all their capabilities and potential. In laying such a foundation, the love each partner has for the other is of great importance.

If we are to develop a mature love, a basic attitude we must foster in ourselves is not to expect anything from our partner. If I don't expect anything from my partner, I am relaxed and can help both of us. By loving my partner in a mature way, I can learn a lot about myself.

Fromm summarizes the concept of mature love particularly well:

Infantile love follows the principle: '*I love because I am loved.*'
Mature love follows the principle: '*I am loved because I love.*'
Immature love says: '*I love you because I need you.*' Mature love
says: '*I need you because I love you.*'[1]

When the attraction between two people takes the form of
an unhealthy emotional dependence, it is very difficult, if
not impossible, for each person to get to know the true character of the other. Such an attachment blinds us and
encourages us to keep the relationship alive, while we ignore
all the signs that tell us that our behaviour, and that of our
partner, is immature and irresponsible.

It is detachment that enables us to understand the character of others. Detachment is, in itself, a sign of spiritual
maturity. Detachment does not mean being cold or distant
but rather means being relatively free, in our feelings and
thoughts, from the domination and influence of others. It is
possible to be strongly attracted to someone and at the same
time to be detached in a spiritual sense. Such detachment
preserves our personal identity and enables us to understand
that we cannot always know all our own motives or those of
others. Detachment gives us strength, independence and
stability and allows us to know ourselves. We must be
responsible, above all, for our own selves, as we can give to
another only what we ourselves already possess. If we feel
invisible, inadequate and a victim of circumstances, then we
will not be able to give anyone else the security and strength
they need.

In a letter written on his behalf, Shoghi Effendi stated:

Each of us is responsible for one life only, and that is our
own . . . the task of perfecting our own life and character is
one that requires all our attention, our will-power and
energy. If we allow our attention and energy to be taken up
in efforts to keep others right and remedy their faults, we
are wasting precious time. We are like ploughmen each of

whom has his team to manage and his plough to direct, and in order to keep his furrow straight he must keep his eye on his goal and concentrate on his own task. If he looks to this side and that to see how Tom and Harry are getting on and to criticize their ploughing, then his own furrow will assuredly become crooked.[2]

Schopenhauer compares the human condition to that of two hedgehogs trying to live through a very severe winter. They dig a den but, as it is very cold even there, they seek warmth and company by snuggling together. However, the closer they get to one another, the more they prick each other with their sharp bristles. Wounded and irritable, they separate once more and again they feel the cold and the loneliness. They try to get close to one another again but once more they hurt each other. They keep on trying and in the end they learn to keep just far enough away from one another not to prick each other too much yet close enough to warm and give each other comfort. If we don't want to end up suffering or dying of cold in our emotional isolation, we, like the hedgehogs, need to learn to live together, side by side, without invading each other's privacy.

An Oriental proverb says, 'If you tie the feet of two birds together, neither can fly although they have four wings.' In a love relationship, the partners need to be united rather than tied together. If each one feels that he or she is a strong and complete person, then it will be easier for them to have a close and intimate relationship. Only by continuing to grow side by side can each person hope and have the certainty that the two will go forward together.

We must accept that our partner, to grow, may need something other than what we think is good for his or her development. This is an aspect of love. In his book *The Prophet*, Kahlil Gibran describes ideal love:

Love one another, but make not a bond of love:
    Let it rather be a moving sea between the shores of
        your souls.
    Fill each other's cup but drink not from one cup.
    Give one another of your bread but eat not from the
        same loaf.
    Sing and dance together and be joyous, but let each
        one of you be alone,
    Even as the strings of a lute are alone though they
        quiver with the same music.

Give your hearts, but not into each other's keeping.
    For only the hand of Life can contain your hearts.
    And stand together yet not too near together:
    For the pillars of the temple stand far apart,
    And the oak tree and the cypress grow not in each
        other's shadow.[3]

Love is all-embracing. If a person loves only one other and is indifferent to everyone else, he is not expressing love but attachment. The vast majority of people believe that it is precisely the exclusive attachment to one person which is the proof of true love, that loving no one but one's partner is the most solid proof of the intensity of one's love. Love, however, is a spiritual quality and is inexhaustible.

We are all capable of great love – much more than we think – and of loving many more people than those to whom we are most closely attached. Loving others does not halve or diminish what we have to give our partner. On the contrary, the more love we can experience, the more love we can share, the more we improve inside. When we dedicate ourselves to an intimate and close relationship with our partner, the intensification of our feelings towards this one individual does not negate the quality of our love for others but rather enriches it. By developing our capacity to love and to extend our love – this spiritual quality – to a wider circle, we renew and intensify the special ties that bind us to our partner.

Those who can only love one person usually have serious problems. They usually want absolute power over the other person, to have control of that person. Not only is this impossible, it is also undesirable. Such an attitude is not a sign of love. It can, in fact, destroy what we think we are protecting. Mary Cholmondeley said that every day she becomes more convinced that our lives are wasted in the love we haven't given, in the powers we haven't used, in our selfish prudence that leads us to avoid any risks. By trying to avoid pain, we also give up our chances of happiness.

Thinking beyond ourselves – focusing on other people's problems and on the world in which we live – is the highest expression of love. It may seem a paradox, but when we think further than ourselves, we can actually see ourselves more clearly. When we love someone, our happiness comes from the awareness that we are the source of their happiness.

7

Mutual Support, Communication and Encouragement

> *A plant will love the soil*
> *in which it grows in harmony.*

Support

How useful support is! It is the medicine for all our ills, holding us up when we feel weak. We need support particularly when we are about to give up, when we are frightened and plagued by doubts and sadness. The support of another, especially our partner, is the only life belt that can help us survive the stormy sea that is our life at that particular time. Such support is especially helpful when we feel there is no way out of our difficulties, when we see all doors closed and there seems to be no way forward. The support of our partner provides the only opening in a dark room, letting in a bit of light and giving us the hope and courage to continue, as we know we are not alone.

If we have a relationship based on love, we can be open and honest with our partner without fear of being judged and knowing that support will be extended to us. We are sure that our partner is our best friend and will, whatever

happens, always help us. Where there is love in our relationship, we can allow ourselves certain liberties: the liberty to
get angry now and again, or even to lose control without
fearing that a permanent scar will be left; the liberty to be
imperfect; the liberty to make a fool of ourselves without
losing the respect of our partner; the liberty to change and to
grow and also to make mistakes without fearing that we will
be abandoned at our moment of greatest need or that we
may be subjected to a barrage of recriminations and judge-
ments, the worst of which is undoubtedly 'I told you so!'

We need support particularly when the worst side of our
character is exposed to our partner. It is just at this time that
the acceptance and affection of our partner become the main-
stays of our life. To preserve our personal dignity, we all need
to feel the warmth and approval of someone we love and
respect.

Communication

All of us need to be shown affection; it is an indispensable
element of growth. Without affection we would die. Affection can be shown without any words being spoken. There
has been much speculation about communication through
thought, extra-sensory perception and so on. Couples,
however, can often develop a form of communication, not
of thoughts but of affection and warmth. If this were developed further, by just looking at another person we could
communicate all our feelings of tenderness, love, understanding and interest. We would not feel so awkward and ill
at ease, shy or aggressive in the presence of others. No one
would be denied the substance of life that makes us grow
and develop just because he was unable to communicate his
needs to others.

If we could demonstrate to others our feelings rather
than give them rational arguments, if we could share our

spiritual emotions instead of our unshakable opinions, then we could develop a feeling of empathy with anyone, even with people who are very different from us in their education, culture, upbringing and sensitivities – how much more so with our partner. If we could overcome our loneliness, sadness, fears and doubts by simply hugging another person in a warm physical and spiritual gesture, many of our problems would disappear like snow melting in the sunshine.

We should practise communicating with our partner not just through words and formal gestures but through a genuine contact of souls; communicating not through our minds but through our hearts; not through rational thought and logic but through something less tangible and more spiritual.

If we want to remove a ball from an iron ring on the floor and it is impossible to move it sideways on the horizontal plane, the solution is to lift the ball up vertically into space, changing the plane of our activity. Here the ball represents our way of communicating. If every time we found it difficult to communicate with another person we simply changed our plane of reference, from the material to the spiritual, we could come together and understand each other on that plane.

Encouragement

Sincere and positive encouragement is much more effective than the continuous criticisms to which we are always ready to subject our loved ones. Negative criticism has a depressing effect and, as time goes by, it actually worsens the negative attitude we want to correct. G. T. Smith said that if we treat people for what they are, they will remain as they are, but, if we treat them as they could be or could become, they will bring out the best in themselves.

It is very important for couples to accept their differences. Nature provides an infinite variety of plants and they are all fascinating. We know that each species is different and that it would be ridiculous to judge them. We do not criticize plants in our garden for not producing new leaves when, in our opinion, they should. We let them develop as is natural for them and – forced flowers intended for show apart – we allow them to grow and flower at their own rate. It would make sense to do the same with our partner but often our impatience to see him grow and behave in what for us is a reasonable manner prompts us to guide and criticize him. Like a forced flower that blooms out of season, we presume that our partner can and should change himself when we want him to. Often, the best service we can render our loved one is to keep our distance, silently and patiently, but with understanding and hope, gently encouraging him to come out of his shell and share with us all the beauty and love possible.

All of this requires giving, generously. When we think we've already given enough, we usually discover that there is a way we can give even more. Some people think that giving is synonymous with sacrifice, in the most painful sense of the word. We soon discover, however, that giving is the highest expression of power. In the act of giving, we have a feeling of true strength and inner richness. This feeling fills us with joy. For many, giving brings more joy than receiving because it is not considered a deprivation.

When giving support and encouragement, it is essential to accept and love the other person, not only for what he is but also for what he could become – to love his potential. This is not the same thing as trying to change him in some way. We must support and encourage our partner without trying to alter his life. Love in this sense is then conceived as an interest in the life and growth of those to whom we are attached. If this interest is lacking, then there is no love.

Love is contagious. Loving is a force that produces love and, as a result, a joy for living. It is certainly true, of course, that in the process of growth we may sometimes feel lost or go through periods when we don't feel up to the task before us. It is then that the encouragement and support provided by a loving partner can see us through.

Thus we go on our journey through life hand in hand, as old friends and good companions, following Camus's advice: 'Don't walk in front of me, I might not follow you; don't walk behind me, I might not be your guide; walk beside me and just be my friend.' On our journey through life together, we will notice the changes in one another but our love will make such changes seem insignificant, for, as Buscaglia reminds us, love allows us to be more comfortable with our mutual imperfections, enabling us to accept them more easily. We will not be so concerned if we begin to get wrinkles on our face, if our skin is more flabby than it was or we develop a pot belly. When we love, our gaze goes beyond these irrelevant things. We concentrate on inner beauty, which is unaffected by time or age.

Love, then, is not blind – it just sees the essentials.

8

Special Moments Together

*Love is not just something we feel,
it is also something we do.*

Marta and Gianni had never spent any time alone together. There was always someone in the house, always some relative or friend visiting. This situation had begun shortly after their marriage and had continued from then on without either one of them objecting. Perhaps they had an unconscious fear of having to communicate with each other or of discovering that they did not really like one another other all that much and that they had chosen the wrong partner. Perhaps it was out of fear of true intimacy, which requires times for reflection and solitude. Their relationship was more like people living together under the same roof than a marriage. Then the marriage broke up, much to everyone's surprise, as to outsiders things seemed to be going well. But when was this couple really married?

Most of us live in watertight compartments. Our lives and interests are split up into well defined sectors: friendship is separated from love, the role of wife from that of mother, work from religion, and ethics and morality from the daily struggle to get through life. When partners have a child, they often forget they are a couple and identify themselves completely with their new role as parents. Similarly, a couple may forget that before they married they were friends, had fun and confided in one another.

When we move from one role to another, we may not realize that we need not – or even should not – abandon our old role completely. Many husbands think they can only really enjoy themselves with their pals playing cards or that they can only talk about sport, politics and the economy with their friends or colleagues, not with their wives. The same applies of course to a wife, who may confide only in her best friend and share certain interests only with a close circle of female friends.

Many circumstances of our daily routine make us fall into habits and certain patterns of activity. We take some things for granted and don't notice that this is happening. Slowly, we get into a rut and convince ourselves that we have no other alternatives or any opportunity to change. For example, many couples are resigned to the fact that they cannot have an evening alone, simply because they have small children. They find all sorts of excuses, saying that for the present they have no time for playing at young lovers and that there will be plenty of time for this when the children are grown up. However, inevitably and relentlessly, years pass and the two still find no time for each other. When, at last, the moment comes that they do have time, they look at each other like strangers and don't know what to do with all their free evenings.

It is essential that couples find time to be alone together, to talk, to keep in touch, to share their feelings. One woman, happily married for over 50 years, gives this advice to newly married couples: 'Spend at least two hours every two weeks alone together. Get a baby sitter for the children and go to the movies or out for dinner; if you have no money, go for a walk and talk; but go as a couple, by yourselves!'[1]

Once they have children, many couples no longer use their first names with each other but use functional substitutes instead such as 'mum' or 'dad'. When this stage has passed, and the children have left home, they may continue to use these terms, feeling it strange to call one another by their names again.

An essential component of forging a couple from two people is their desire to have fun together and their willingness to confide in one another. Of all the relationships we may have and enter into during our lifetime, the most important is the one we have with our partner, that very special person who should be our friend, companion, confident and the keeper of our secrets; someone who, in good times and bad, does not leave us on our own and to whom we can turn at any time, because we know he is loyal, honest and always there to help.

Our attitude should be that each day is a new day and every morning is like the beginning of a new life. We might well think of every morning as if it were our birthday. If we look carefully at 12 June, for instance, we see that, in itself, it is the same as any other day of the year; it is only special because of a particular meaning we have given to it. It is we who give it this meaning, so it is possible to give every day meaning. Someone once said: 'Life is a gift, but the quality of life is a choice.'

Nowadays, we are used to taking everything very seriously and confusing this with maturity and proper behaviour, and we think that by doing so we are wiser. For instance, at a meeting with his son's mathematics teacher, a parent was told that the boy was rather immature because he was always cheerful! In the relationship of a married couple, cheerfulness and a sense of humour can be very useful and should be developed, as should the imagination necessary to have fun together.

'Please, dear, don't insist! We can't go on seeing each other in secret and catching the same train every day!' 'Young lady, will you stop making advances to me! People are staring at us.' The first of these statements was made

49

one morning in a very crowded underground station, the second on a bus in a large city on another morning. People overhearing the conversations must have thought that the couple were lovers or at least strange in some way; rather, the couple had been married for years. Such jokes are very embarrassing at the time but they can be funny and they demonstrate the couple's vivacity and their desire to enjoy life together.

Unfortunately, many more couples will identify with this sad poem by Lois Wyse:

So many TV marriages.
Acting our lives out against
the background of a television screen.
Instead of two lives in a room,
there are two lives and the 11 o'clock news
with regular breaks for commercials.
Instead of what you say and what I say
there's what Dick and John and their guests say.

You don't laugh with me,
I don't laugh with you.
All the fun comes out of the screen.
And we laugh about it together.
The more we avoid talking to each other
the more our relationship becomes passive.
Television lets us go through life
playing minor supporting roles.
And the less we talk
the harder it is for us to talk.

9

Developing Goals, Realizing Potential

We cannot choose how and when we will die,
but we can decide how we will live.

A poet once said that love is not gazing into each other's eyes but rather gazing in the same direction. Among the factors that keep a couple together are their shared vision of life and having common ideals. Developing a shared vision is one of the goals of marriage.

The essence of love is working for something and cultivating it. It is important to understand that love and work go together. This means knowing what your aim is in life, setting goals and having a clear vision of your future. Working to achieve a goal brings real happiness.

A married couple may have many goals and plans for the future. These plans will no doubt include the development and strengthening of the marriage itself, the growth of both partners as individuals and the development of their potential, the education and nurturing of the children of the family and the security of the family. If we understand that marriage is a 'fortress for well-being and salvation',[1] and heed the advice of Bahá'u'lláh to 'Build ye for yourselves such houses as the rain and floods can never destroy, which shall protect you from the changes and chances of this life'[2], we have the framework within which we can plan and build a secure future as a couple.

In order to achieve a goal, we must know what it is and how to get to it. It is like driving to a remote village. We must start where we are and follow the road signs. If we follow the signs, slowly but surely we will get to where we want to go. It is not enough just to *say* what we are going to do, although this is positive in itself. We must *act*. As a Buddhist teacher once said: 'Knowing and not doing is the same as not knowing.' We are what we do. Good intentions that remain only as intentions are of no use to anyone.

We come into this world ignorant and unaware. Our main task, the real goal of our life, is to leave it in a state of knowledge. To do this we must recognize that we have potential which we must develop and cultivate.

There is nothing more dangerous than standing still. Everything must grow and develop or die. Charles Dubois says that the important thing is always to be able to sacrifice what we are for what we could become. The foetus develops all its limbs inside its mother's womb so that it can be born into this world as a complete human being and progress satisfactorily. We are born into this world so that we may develop all our spiritual 'limbs', such as love, justice, honesty and humility, and may leave this world as complete as possible to continue our spiritual evolution in the next. The human being should strive to be like the earth itself and develop its three fundamental characteristics: trustworthiness – you can hide a treasure in the earth and when you go back you will find it intact; creativity, or fertility – if you sow a seed, the earth gives you in return thousands of seeds and their fruits; humility – humanity walks all over the earth but the earth is not destroyed; rather, it supports and bears every burden.

Bahá'u'lláh says we are a mine of priceless gems and a jewel-box containing the most precious stones.[3] Education and awareness of the aim of life are the keys we can use to open this jewel-box of our potential.

Awareness of our true purpose and goal should guide every thought and action in our lives. It should be reflected in our marriage and in the upbringing of our children. If our goal is to develop spiritual qualities, then one goal of marriage is to help each partner to do this.

God has given each of us a sort of container and we can put into it whatever we like. Everything we potentially are is positive and full of light. Even in the world around us, everything that is negative, evil or unilluminated is so only because of the absence of the positive, goodness and light. The more we fill our container with positive values, and the greater the care we take in doing so, the smoother and more peaceful our journey through life will be.

As as well giving everyone the opportunity to develop and grow, God has also given each person particular abilities and potential. It is as if some received a bag, some a case and others a trunk. The quantity of our abilities and opportunities is not important but the effort and good will we put into filling our containers are. It is obvious that someone who has received a bag and fills it almost completely feels more satisfied than the person who fills up only half of his trunk. If our goal is to realize our potential as an individual, then one purpose of our marriage is to help one another develop that potential. For a marriage to thrive and develop, each partner must be aware of his or her own essence, potential and aim in life. The partners must then work together and share their visions of life and their plans. The partners in the marriage can thus help one another to develop their potential and to contribute to their process of growth, remembering that we can give only what we have, or rather, what we are.

10

The Spiritual Bond

*Moral and spiritual values
do not limit, but protect.*

Rita is a typical romantic woman who places a lot of importance on physical details. For her, whether a person is nice or not depends on her perfume. Gestures, words and tone of voice all have a particular meaning for Rita. Rita's husband Lorenzo is uncomplicated, happy-go-lucky and a bit gullible. Rita's intuition is such that she immediately grasps things that Lorenzo doesn't even come close to understanding. Rita often daydreams and deep down she is happier in her own world of thoughts and fantasies than in the reality of everyday life, which she finds boring and depressing.

Routine, which Rita hates, puts Lorenzo at ease. No shocks, no surprises, nothing new: that's how he likes things. When Rita talks about candlelight dinners she has a sparkle in her eye. Lorenzo also talks about sparks but only those from the sparkplugs that have to be checked on his car. Rita and Lorenzo are very different but are united by a deep affection. They used to worry that their paths might someday divide, so at a certain point in their lives they decided to try to understand each other better. They began by first glancing at and then looking deeply into their different worlds. They found pleasant and unexpected aspects in their differences and enjoyed the experience of this new life together.

Sometimes in a marriage we feel that our bodies are not united but that there is contact between our souls. This happens only very rarely and this is perhaps why such moments are so precious that they cannot easily be described: they can only be cherished in our hearts. Such contact generally does not take place when we are distracted by our many day-to-day problems or when our hearts and minds are at ease. More often such spiritual connections take place at times of great suffering and difficulty. It is as if our souls come out into the light and are confronted by a different reality.

Think, for example, of the unity a married couple feels when there is a death in the family. No words, no particular gestures or demonstrations of feelings are needed. They simply cry together. Nothing unites hearts more than tears shed together. Tears at such times are like spring showers that wash everything away, all the dust that has gathered on our souls. Afterwards, we see reality in a clearer light and, perhaps, for a short time, we may even see ourselves reflected in the image of the other person.

Spiritual bonding can be stimulated and helped to grow. As a couple we might reflect together on our own existence, on our life so far and on the age-old themes of life: the mysteries of birth, life and death; why 'man is not aware of being born, why he suffers when he dies and yet forgets to live'. We can pray together, prayers that are not merely wishes to be fulfilled but simple acts of thanksgiving for the peace of the moment, for the gift of love received. 'Together make mention of noble aspiration and heavenly concepts,' 'Abdu'l-Bahá advises.[1]

For many couples, experiencing together the birth of their child is an occasion when spiritual unity is forged: the kisses, the caresses and the intimate looks exchanged at this moment are nothing like the affectionate gestures made at other times.

Spiritual unity might be found in a warm, comforting embrace in which no words are spoken and which has no sexual undertones. Such gestures of affection give us strength and reassure us that we are loved and accepted.

Periods of suffering experienced together help us grow and mature and can also be occasions when partners share a strong spiritual bond. As someone once said, 'Difficulties are the shortest way to our goals.' By accepting and experiencing unexpected events together we can discover the hidden wisdom in everything that happens to us.

Often in difficult situations we falter in our attempt to achieve a certain solution. Then, suddenly, with the help of our partner, the answer becomes obvious. It's like what happens to a swimmer when the sea suddenly becomes rough. He calls upon all his strength and swims until he is exhausted and, just when he's beginning to think he won't make it, his foot touches the bottom and he knows he's safe at last. There is always a friendly wave that washes us ashore. This is achieved because there is a spiritual bond between partners.

These are just a few examples. Every couple has intimate and very private experiences which bring them closer together and through which they feel more united.

One of the qualities of the soul is its deep-felt desire to *belong*, to belong to somebody – ultimately, of course, to God. We are not islands and it is definitely not good for a person to be alone. By nurturing our spiritual bonds, we feel we belong to one another and can face any storm. 'Nourish continually', 'Abdu'l-Bahá tells us, 'the tree of your union with love and affection, so that it will remain ever green and verdant throughout all seasons and bring forth luscious fruits for the healing of nations.'[2]

One way for a married couple to experience great intimacy

and union is to meditate together, for example on this beautiful poetic image:

> If you want to see the valleys,
> > climb to the top of the mountain.
> If you want to see the top of the mountain,
> > rise above the clouds.
> But if you want to understand the clouds,
> > close your eyes and think.

11

Interchangeable and Flexible Roles

*We are capable of offering much
but rarely do we excel in our
ability to make small sacrifices.*
Johann Wolfgang von Goethe

'I've put some sauce and a roast in the freezer. You can take your shirts to the dry cleaners or to my mother's. On Tuesday, you can have lunch at your mother's. So, in the five days I'm away, you should be able to manage!'

Who's speaking and what's happening? You will probably guess that it is a wife who is going to be away from home. She's going into hospital to have a baby. So closely identified is she with the organization of her home and all domestic matters – even though she also has a job – that her husband has become like a person who is so disabled that without her preparations he would not be able to survive in the mysterious world that is his own home. He needs a guidebook just to find a pair of socks or the coffee or sugar. The washing machine and the other electrical appliances are to him diabolical contraptions that only his wife, with her long experience, can use without causing disasters or flooding the flat and transforming it into a miniature Noah's ark.

At the same time, it may be that the wife has never been interested in the macroeconomics of the couple's life and without her partner could not renew the house insurance, pay the bills without spending all the money they have in the bank or avoid paying a penalty for allowing a licence to expire.

Obviously, many couples do share household tasks and everyday matters but not everyone is capable of doing every task. The most important thing for the enrichment of our personal experience is that roles should not be so fixed or so rigid that we find ourselves in difficult situations when our partner is not around. The more we broaden our horizons, the more experience we get, the more roles we will be able to take on and the richer our life will become. The joy a father experiences when he bathes his small child is, for most men, considerably more satisfying than taking the car to be washed.

During the first period of their life together, a couple naturally acquire new habits and divide household chores. In many marriages, tradition is allowed to dictate that certain tasks are assigned to the woman. In such marriages, the man who helps his wife often feels that he is being very good, considerate and generous. The husband tells himself that he is *helping* and *participating*. But he is not really *sharing*. 'I'll take out the rubbish for you,' he says, as if the rubbish belonged only to his wife. 'I'll wash the dishes for you,' he offers, as if the plates were her personal property.

If the roles of men and women can become flexible and interchangeable, domestic tasks will become of secondary importance and cease to be a battlefield. Cultural traditions need not be followed in the division of labour and opportunities in the home. None of us is born with a specific function in life. There is nothing in our DNA that makes us able to wash up better than someone else. We are the air we breathe. If our parents do not know how to speak any other language than Norwegian, then we will learn that language as a child living in their home. The same goes for feelings and attitudes. Many children learn to say 'no' before 'yes' because they hear it more often. If a child hears only the singing of Pavarotti, it is for him like hearing nursery rhymes is for another. It is all a question of learning what the home offers. In a letter written on his behalf, Shoghi Effendi said that 'It is often difficult for us to do things because they are so very different from what we are used to, not because the thing itself is particularly difficult.'[1] In a marriage, we must be open to learning a variety of tasks that our partner may usually undertake and train ourselves to learn something from everyone.

At the same time, in our relationship as a couple, we should never oblige our partner – or our children, for that matter – to do something for us in the name of love. Love is not bargaining.

12

Equality of Women and Men

Do not oppress one another;
no one can grow in the shade.

When it came to the house and children, Luigi was never around. Sara organized and controlled everything. Then, one day, Luigi lost his job and had to stay at home – and he didn't like what he found. Sara told him that if he wanted to have a say in family matters then he had to lend a hand with the work, share the household responsibilities and do his part in bringing up the children. 'You are entitled to your rights only if you recognize your obligations,' she told him. 'You can't be an armchair critic. You must get actively involved.' Luigi finally understood and for the first time since he had been married, he began to get involved in family life. Thus he earned the right to have his say in things.

Mahatma Gandhi said that if he had been born a woman, he would have rebelled against men's assumption that women are born to be the objects of their pleasure. He decided to treat his wife completely differently from the way he had previously, restoring to her the rights he had taken away and renouncing the rights he had acquired as her husband. As Mahatma Gandhi saw, the possibility of building a sound relationship as a couple depends on our capacity to base the relationship on equality. A sound relationship can be created only between two people who feel themselves to be of equal worth.

This has far-reaching implications for the attitudes and behaviours of both men and women. For example, men will need to learn to express their emotions and understand this as something necessary for the development of every human being. It has been said that if men cried more there would be fewer wars. Men will need to learn to ask for help, to be maternal, to cooperate and overcome conflicts peacefully and also to accept attitudes and kinds of behaviour that traditionally have been considered feminine.

A woman, it has been said, knows a man and his needs better than she knows herself, as her upbringing and culture have conditioned her from a very young age to look after others. Men also need to have this sort of upbringing if we want them to know the 'other half of heaven' better.

After centuries of discrimination against them, the time has come to give women priority in education and opportunity. For how long? Until equality between women and men is established and secured. Men have unique responsibilities and will obtain great benefits when their equality with women is finally achieved. The task of men today is to encourage women, to guarantee their rights and not to persist in drawing attention to their own needs as males. For example, men should not prevent or restrict the entry of women into a job by setting requirements for candidates based on tradition.

Believing in the principle of equality is the first step to achieving it. It means, above all, looking within ourselves and examining our relationships with others so that we can put this principle into practice in our everyday, personal life. The first test of equality is the willingness of men to let women talk. Women, on the other hand, do not have to compete with men in every field. A frank and open dialogue between women and men, carried out with patience, will inevitably lead to changes in individuals and in society. We should eliminate conflict and argument but this does not mean that we should avoid examining the many problems of a historical, psychological, economic and social nature that have blighted the relationship between women and men through the ages. Neither does it mean that women, in their effort to establish the principle of equality, should wait until everyone is ready to accept it.

Humankind is evolving from its adolescence into maturity and, just as a mature individual abandons the habits and attitudes typical of adolescence, so too must humanity modify those aspects of its culture that are no longer suitable for a more mature age. It is not easy to change a culture in which patriarchy has been dominant for thousands of years. Badinter says that men today, having been forced to abandon their role as patriarchs, must re-invent the father figure and the virility that goes with it while women await these changes with baited breath.

At the moment, men have a very difficult task. They have inherited attitudes from the past, and although they cannot be blamed for the mistakes of their fathers, they do have the responsibility slowly to shake off this difficult inheritance. The fact that many women are good at looking after the home needs and comforts of the family is no reason for continuing to identify them with a family role exclusively. A hundred and fifty years ago people were led to believe that African-Americans were particularly good at picking cotton and that no white person could compete with them in this activity. The aim was merely to maintain the *status quo* – slavery. Today, societies all over the world desperately need the qualities of personal sacrifice that women have developed over thousands of years – compassion, altruism, affectionate care and attention, self-denial and, above all, conciliation and peacemaking – yet by and large women are prevented from offering these talents outside the home. The fossilization of roles isolates many women, makes them lonely and prevents them from developing – or causes them to lose – their self-respect. This, in turn, means they may not be able to take advantage of the opportunities becoming available to them outside the home. This situation is of no advantage to anyone and transmits behaviour patterns that will be of no help to the future development of our children.

The identity of a person should be separated from the role he or she plays in life. For centuries society has divided people on the basis of their roles: engineers, labourers, homemakers, etc. We must now help one another to rediscover our own selves and to view each other independently of the roles we play in society, to come to know one another through the complementarity of various attributes, some of which may be described as female and others as male.

Each of us has a different temperament and style from anyone else and this is our particular contribution to the world. How monotonous it would be if everyone expressed themselves in the same way. It is our differences that make us interesting. Some of us are impulsive and take risks while others prefer to take things more slowly. Some are very sociable while others prefer to be alone. Some people are spontaneous and others are more reflective. There are those who go into everything boldly and others who are more careful. There are perfectionists and those who are content to make do. We will encounter these differences in our relationship and we should make an effort not to impose our values on a partner who may have a different behaviour pattern from our own. Our love should leave sufficient breathing space for each of us. So long as we are open to diversity in all our relationships, we will continue to enrich our personalities. In this world, there are as many ways of relating to life as there are human beings. Because everyone has within himself a different world and universe to be discovered, the more frequent and different our contacts are, the richer and greater our capacity to love will become.

We live in a culture of fear: fear of what is different, fear of what is new and, therefore, unknown, and fear of our surroundings. By keeping in touch with one another – communicating – and exploring new situations together, we will not be afraid of the differences we may encounter along the road to mutual knowledge. Variety is a source of richness and beauty, as we see in a garden of different flowers with their different colours and perfumes. Being different from one another does not mean that we are divided. Rather diversity enables us better to appreciate the unique qualities of others. Unity in diversity is the basic law of the universe.

13

In-Laws

You're just like your mother!
You're all the same in your family!

When we say that society is made up of individuals this is not quite true. We should say that society is *built up* by individuals, as it is not by putting various people together that a society is formed. A crowd at a concert or in a stadium can certainly not be called a society. A society exists only if relationships and ties among individuals also exist.

The same applies to people of different ages living together in the same home. We say that the family is the basis of society but we cannot talk about a family if no bonds exist among the individual members. The basic determinant of our family life is, therefore, the quantity and quality of our relationships.

As a person goes through life he or she goes through several fundamental stages such as birth, adolescence – the transition from childhood to adulthood – adulthood, pairing with another person and forming a couple, giving life to a child. Each of these stages involves moments of great joy and gratification as well as periods of stress and suffering. The stage in which two individuals form a relationship and become a couple can be particularly challenging. The couple must give much thought to the process and take care to learn something of each other's character.

When we are thinking about marrying, one of the best ways to get to know the character of our prospective partner is to examine his relationship with his parents, as people often follow the pattern offered to them by their own families. This does not mean that we should base our evaluation only on the existence or otherwise of an idyllic relationship between our partner and his own parents. On the contrary, we should try to discover the level of mutual respect that exists, the solidarity of the family and whether the family practices unity in diversity.

A strong attachment to our partner often prevents us from getting to know certain aspects of his character. It is, therefore, important to observe our future partner in his relationships with others and to learn what kind of people his intimate friends are. Anyone who is incapable of treating other people in a kind and polite way will probably not be able to show respect and kindness at home to his partner or to his children. Demonstrations of possessiveness, greed, jealousy and arrogance are all signs of immaturity, although we may mistake them for signs of great love for us. If we observe these attributes in our partner's relationship with his own family, it is likely that they will be repeated when he marries.

It is important for partners to meet and come to know each other's families for another reason: in marriage it is not just two individuals who come together but rather two whole families. When we marry, not only do we unite with another individual and his or her personal cultural and educational background, we also establish ties and relationships with our partner's entire family. This aspect of marriage should not be neglected, as it often influences the couple's relationship and their ultimate harmony.

After a couple marry the relationships they form with their respective in-laws may well determine the health and harmony of their own marriage. All good relationships depend on good communication and this is particularly true of the relationship we have with our in-laws. It is worth spending time developing good communications with our in-laws and giving our relationship with them much attention. Each partner must develop respect for the parents and family members of his spouse. Such mutual respect for parents and relatives, of course, should not go beyond certain limits, such as accepting interference in the way we as a couple live our lives.

14

Thinking Positively

*Life can be marvellous,
even if reality is not.*

Gibran said that the optimist sees the rose and not the thorns, while the pessimist sees only the thorns and forgets the rose. It is not the thing observed or its condition that changes. What changes is our attitude.

In present day society, a person, right from birth, becomes used to having his mistakes pointed out. For most children, punishment plays a larger part in their lives than rewards, partly because their parents' attention is drawn more to negative situations. When the child goes to school, the main task of the teachers seems to be to underline his mistakes with a red pen (and not, metaphorically speaking, highlighting his good work with a green one). Even if the child does well at school, the teacher feels compelled to say, 'You could do better!' The result is that few children ever receive any reward or recognition without 'ifs' and 'buts'. When we leave school, we start work and very few of us find encouragement, support or praise. Here, too, the attention of superiors or colleagues is drawn only to mistakes. Television and the mass media generally focus on bad news, tragedies and catastrophes and cover particularly negative events, leaving us with the impression that misfortune is the only thing worth paying attention to.

As we are immersed in this negative attitude and have grown up more in the shade than in the light, it is often difficult for us to be positive and to see a glass as half full rather than as half empty. Yet it is just this – the need to be optimistic – that is the great challenge in our lives. We must muster all our strength and energy to ignore the rain and the damp and to delight in the colours of autumn, to appreciate the beauty of the snow in winter without thinking of the effort required to clear it, to wonder at the miracle of reawakening nature in the spring without complaining of the allergies that come with it, and to experience the pleasant sensation of the warmth of the summer sun without worrying too much about the gnats. Even the yellow colour of the leaves in autumn can be seen in two different ways: as the colour the leaves have taken from the summer sun to give back to us in autumn or simply as a sign of the withering and approaching death of the leaves.

Fromm explains a number of the attitudes we adopt as adults:

> Motherly love . . . makes the child feel: it is good to have been born; it instils in the child the *love for life*, and not only the wish to remain alive. The same idea may be taken to be expressed in another Biblical symbolism. The promised land (land is always a mother symbol) is described as 'flowing with milk and honey'. Milk is the symbol of the first aspect of love, that of care and affirmation. Honey symbolizes the sweetness of life, the love for it and the happiness in being alive. Most mothers are capable of giving 'milk', but only a minority of giving 'honey' too. In order to be able to give 'honey', a mother must not only be a 'good mother', but a happy person – and this aim is not achieved by many. The effect on the child can hardly be exaggerated. Mother's love for life is as infectious as her

74

anxiety is. Both attitudes have a deep effect on the child's whole personality: one can distinguish indeed, among children – and adults – those who got only 'milk' and those who got both 'milk and honey.'[1]

We live in a world full of sceptics and cynics. They consider themselves to be particularly realistic and do all they can to highlight the wickedness and moral dishonesty that they think are the natural essence of man. They are convinced that every act of generosity and kindness has an ulterior motive and that nobody does anything unless he gets something in return. It is much easier to become cynical and critical in negative situations than to act and fight to improve things.

One of the worst things we can do to our children is to rob them of their future and their hope by burdening them with our negative experiences. Taking the smile and the hope away from someone is certainly the worst of crimes but there seems to be no punishment for it. How many times have I seen the light go out in the eyes of a young person when some middle-aged man expressed opinions against which the youth had no argument, only dreams. Someone will always say, 'Dreams are not enough.' Michelles de Saint Pierre observed that an optimist can always see the light if there is any but wondered why pessimists always rush to turn it out. We all need something to look forward to that is better than the present. We need to believe that perfection is possible but also have the courage to be imperfect.

Like a sailor who steers by the stars, we follow the path of our life with its ups and downs and bends. It can be dangerous at times. Some stretches are dark while others are brightly lit. There may also be fog banks alternating with sunny spells and thunderstorms followed by rainbows. The skilled and optimistic sailor sails through all these conditions; the pessimistic one turns back at the first storm.

Pain and suffering can either renew a person or destroy him. We should accept pain and suffering as natural conditions of existence, as essential elements of growth, but not be resigned to them. Rather we should learn from pain and suffering. There is no birth without labour. We often become more mature and wise through the failures and difficulties in our lives than through our successes. A situation that at the time seems impossible to live through, which causes us to suffer the torments of hell, can, once it has been experienced and overcome, leave us more mature and freer than we were before.

Kafka said that whoever retains the capacity to appreciate beauty will never grow old. The reverse of this also seems to be true. If we continue to say that things will go badly for us, the probability is that things will go badly, exactly as we expect. Shakespeare said that beauty and ugliness as such do not exist. Rather, it is our thoughts and attitudes that make something beautiful or ugly. If we concentrate on constructive images that enrich our relationships, we free ourselves from the images of the past and are more aware of and encouraged by the present. As a result, we are less afraid.

Fear paralyses us, while courage enables us to progress. To overcome fear, we need courage. But how can we find it? An effective method is to be more positive in our attitude towards life and our view of things. When we observe something negative, we should remember that there are always two sides to everything and that it is always possible to find the good side.

Another feeling that can paralyse us is guilt. As we grow and develop, we often feel lost or go through periods when we don't feel up to the task before us, or feel that we haven't given enough, or that we weren't there when we were needed. It is then that our sense of guilt, a negative feeling that makes us suffer, comes to the surface. This seems to be particularly true for women. I suspect that when the sense of guilt was being handed out at the beginning of creation, women were in the front of the queue and got most of it. However, a sense of guilt does us no good, as it forces us to look backwards, to pity ourselves and, therefore, to remain where we are. It is the opposite of optimism and thinking positively. Dreikurs wrote, 'Guilt feelings are the expression of good intentions that we do not have at all'.[2] On the other hand, a sense of shame for something we have done wrong is an unpleasant but useful experience as it means we have already suffered enough, can put right what we can, and can start again with a clean slate.

The people who are unhappy because they lack superfluous things far outnumber those who are unhappy because they lack necessities. Generally, a person who is not happy with what he has would not be happy even with what he would like to have.

Experience shows that if we really want to make our dreams come true, we can do so. A person who loves and has a positive attitude never stops trying and never gives in. He will do everything he can to get the best out of life and to transform his dreams into reality.

We reach the top of a mountain only after a great effort – usually having grazed our hands and knees – but we are more than recompensed for our efforts by the view we have of the infinite horizon, a view that fills us with joy and amazement. The higher we climb a mountain, the wider the horizon becomes. The view becomes more spectacular and the number of things we discover increases.

We should not use up all our energy in trying to change those aspects of our lives that cannot be altered but rather work hard to change our attitude to them. For example, I have to go out and it's raining. I don't want to get wet but I can't change the weather and make the rain stop. I can, however, put on a raincoat and take my umbrella.

In this context it is useful to recall this well-known prayer:

O God, give me the courage to change the things I can change, the strength to accept the things I cannot change and the wisdom to distinguish between the two.

An example of what changing our attitude means is provided by Sydney Harris, a journalist. One day he went with a friend of his to a newspaper stall. The friend warmly greeted the news agent, who simply replied with a grunt. When the news agent brusquely handed the man a newspaper, Sydney Harris's friend took it and wished the news agent a pleasant weekend. As they walked away along the street, the journalist asked his friend, 'Is that man always so rude to you?'

'Yes, unfortunately.'

'And are you always so polite to him?'

'Yes.'

'Then why are you so polite, if he isn't?'

'Because I don't want to let him decide how I should act.'

A person who is truly human is free, knows how to be himself or herself at every moment, does not give in at the slightest pressure and does not allow his or her own actions and responses to be determined by the mean actions or fits of temper of others. A person who is truly human acts and does not merely react.

A person who loves should do everything possible to banish all negative feelings and to concentrate on beauty, goodness and joy. Although he should remain aware that life is not always easy or happy and that bad things do happen, he should avoid focusing on this. To dwell obsessively on what is bad in this world prevents us from seeing everything that is beautiful and good. We find solutions to problems by keeping as many doors open as possible. Negative people always look for and find the confirmation of their own negative attitude, just as positive people look for and find the good things in life. Both types of people exist: the fundamental difference between them lies in the choices they make. Satisfied and sensitive people who are happy inside have more stable and meaningful relationships.

When it comes to our relationship with our partner, we need to develop this sense of thinking positively. It is important to understand that human beings can change their lives by adopting a different mental attitude. A sense of humour and the capacity to take the heat out of a situation, the ability to enjoy life and to laugh together are all signs of maturity. On the other hand, people who take things for granted, who rarely laugh and who are always moaning are unprepared for a serious and lasting relationship. This is why, when choosing a partner, it is very important to learn all we can about the other person, to observe him or her in different situations. It is possible to judge the maturity of a person by reflecting on how he faces life and its problems, whether he has a negative attitude, is fearful or guilty. If our prospective partner usually faces difficulties by looking for causes elsewhere or avoids discussing or analyzing problems, this sign should not be ignored. We should consider seriously whether this is the right person for us.

15

Sex

Solitude, the feeling of being unwanted,
is the worst kind of poverty.

What a difference there is between a skier who is taking part in a competition and whose main objective is to win by arriving at the bottom in the shortest possible time, and a person who skis just for the pleasure of feeling the snow slide under her feet, the warmth of the sun on her skin, the tingle of the cold air on her face, and the joy and wonder of passing through beautiful scenery. What a difference there is between walking when we are in a hurry and have to move quickly because we have an appointment and don't want to arrive late and just strolling along the same route and stopping to look at the shop windows or to buy an ice cream, enjoying every step because we have no particular destination. We are conditioned by our consumer culture and the mass media to believe that reaching a goal is more important than the path we follow to get there. Even if we remain profoundly ignorant, a certificate stating that we have a particular qualification is seen to be more important than the love of learning and even learning itself. Our whole life is spent running to reach true or imaginary goals.

In our frenetic everyday life, rushing and speed are the driving forces of our existence. We wake up in the morning at the last moment and start our day with a quick wash and a rushed breakfast or perhaps just a cup of coffee. At lunch time, many people now tend to eat a sandwich in a cafe or even at their desks rather than have a light meal in a more peaceful environment. Supper, which for many women means more work, is eaten in front of the television, while perhaps also keeping an eye on the children and reading the post. We finally crash out on the sofa in the company of the people on the TV.

If we suffer with insomnia we have no option but to take a sleeping tablet, whatever it costs us in terms of our health, because we are also in a rush to go to sleep.

This is what life is like for many people, even housewives, who supposedly have more free time as they don't have to clock in to work in the morning. This explains the bad tempers in the queue at the baker's when somebody nips in before somebody else. We are all so conditioned to rushing around that even when we go on an outing, without noticing it we are still in a hurry. We dangerously overtake the car in front of ours, although we have no schedule to keep to, or we eat our lunch quickly, although we have all the time in the world.

Speed has become the dominant theme in our lives. At the rate we live, we waste part of our existence, losing out on the small things that make life special: the beauty of nature that can be seen in one single geranium plant on our window sill; the feelings we can derive from music but not from the noise of the traffic in our cities; the pleasure we get from the smell of freshly printed paper when reading a new book.

Today, we feel we must always be busy and move continuously in many different directions, otherwise we feel uneasy. When we are still we listen to ourselves better and we become more aware of our emotions and our feelings and, sometimes what we feel is not very nice, so we must be continually on the move to avoid listening to ourselves.

Even where sex is involved, nearly all of us rush instead of being ready and willing to take our time and to listen. We think only of the goal and not how we get there. Everything is frenetic and little attention is paid to details. This becomes a great obstacle for the achievement of a problem-free sex life. Where sex is concerned, speed has an enormously negative effect on the evolution of a satisfying sexual relationship.

A person who is truly in love is like a lamp that is lit and gives off a lovely light. He or she is different from a person who is not in love. Such a person may still be a very good lamp but will not give off light or warmth. Many of us look for and are attracted by the shape of the lamp rather than its light, although we are looking for warmth and light.

Some scientists tell us that humans have sexual desires precisely because they have a sex. The truth, however, is the exact opposite. Sartre points out that physiological phenomenon cannot explain or provoke sexual desire just as the constriction of veins or the dilation of pupils cannot explain or provoke fear. Sexual desire is inborn in our minds and is associated with the need for love. Love can make us desire sexual union but it should not to be confused with the desire to conquer, to possess or be conquered. If the desire for physical union is not accompanied by love, sexual attraction creates an illusion of union, but immediately afterwards the partners become two strangers again, divided as before and perhaps with feelings of guilt and disillusion.

Very often two people who are going through a critical period in their lives as a couple use sex as a weapon to hurt or reject, humiliate or cause the estrangement of their partner. If conflicts are not brought into the open, or are perhaps hidden by good manners (imposed more by our upbringing than by a true bond of affection), sexual rejection can remain at an unconscious level. The two people love each other but the desire for sex is just not there. Difficulties in sexual relationships are often nothing more than difficulties of communicating. What we see, therefore, is just the tip of the iceberg. It is generally useless to try to explain or solve sexual problems without delving deeply into the minds of the two people and into the nature of their relationship.

Open dialogue, sincerity, intimacy and the ability to confess one's own weaknesses, limitations, fears and doubts are all necessary to improve a difficult sexual relationship. Often, just a touch, a hug or a loving gesture will give a new lease of life to the physical side of love and will revitalize non-verbal communication between the partners. Demonstrations of kindness and unselfish affection can often become the means for thawing certain situations.

We have all got a lot to learn about sex, as few of us have ever had a real education in sexuality. To educate someone for sex is simply to educate him for life. Sexuality is not static. Like any other form of communication, it is dynamic and should therefore be continuously evolving.

When we are experiencing difficulties in our sex life, it is worth remembering that affection, the main source of life, may sometimes be manifested through a non-sexual contact. By 'affection' I mean that extraordinary source of physical and emotional well-being which is a major component of love and which is so important for a satisfying sex life. Displays of affection give energy and new life to a relationship and have no need for any particular equipment or tools. Affection can be shown through simple actions such as a caress, a smile or a hug. This is within everyone's reach.

16

Communication

Everyone is right,
but the truth belongs to nobody.

'Robert, when does the first performance start?'

'Just make sure you're ready for seven o'clock.'

Lucia asks a simple question requesting information but Robert gives her an answer to a completely different question. This is a perfect example of a failure to communicate – we think we understand one other and are surprised by the negative reaction of the other person. With strangers we are more careful about what we say and try to make sure that the person we are talking to has really understood. Between a husband and wife, however, we take it for granted that a common language is used and interpreted by both in the same way. We never suspect that the meanings we give to words and phrases might not be the same as those given by our partner. Our statements, however, are not just a string of words put together. Rather, they are a reflection of the whole of our lives, experiences and emotions, which are certainly different from those of the person to whom we are talking.

Many women believe that men do not really talk to them but that they merely get on their high horses to criticize them. In turn, many men say that women moan all the time and never get down to the nitty gritty of a problem.

No two people on this earth are exactly alike and this is even more true if they are of opposite sex. Deborah Tannen, a linguist, highlighted these differences in her books.[1] When she looked at notions of friendship, for example, she found that men and women hold very different ideas. Generally, for women, friendship involves sharing secrets and confidential matters. For men, on the other hand, a friend is someone to have a conversation with, to have fun with and to be a companion in sport.

Tannen also found that the word freedom has different connotations for women and men. A survey conducted among divorced couples demonstrated that for women freedom means independence of thought and action, being a free agent and not having to worry any more about a husband's reaction. For a men it means having less responsibility and fewer ties.

Men are generally more at ease talking in public and in large groups. Even with people they hardly know, they usually find something to talk about. Women, on the other hand, love to talk in private, with just a few people they know very well. In these circumstances, many women become very talkative, while men usually look on.

In general, men talk to give information and women to create relationships. At home, men feel they can finally be silent while women feel freer to express themselves. This is the origin of an Italian saying: 'Men give lectures and women confide.'

As a rule, a woman likes to talk, consult and discuss matters with her partner, even about small things or minor decisions in life, from what to wear to a party to events of much greater importance, such as the education of their children. It often does not matter to her what the final decision is, which may be very different from that suggested by her partner. A woman needs to hear her partner's opinion, perhaps to give more weight to a decision she has already made. Men, on the other hand, prefer to decide things on their own, without too much interference. In general, women love to discuss things and reach a consensus, while men hate long discussions over trivial matters and find such conversations make them tired and irritable.

Although every human being needs both independence and intimacy, women generally look more for intimacy, while men seek independence. One wife was particularly offended because her husband had not told her about a large sum of money he had spent. She would never have done this without consulting him first. For the husband, the idea of having to inform his wife first was like having to ask for her permission and this meant he was not a free agent and did not have the freedom to do what he wanted. The wife, on the other hand, took it for granted that a couple should discuss their plans, as their two lives were bound up together and the actions of one influenced and had consequences for the other. For her, this was not a burden. On the contrary, she liked to think of her life as being closely linked with her partner's.

Although we have focused on the existence of different languages and attitudes of men and women, it is certainly not the case that it is impossible for the two sexes to communicate. On the contrary, knowing another language enriches our whole being and helps us understand and express ourselves better. In a relationship, communication between two people is like a tennis match. If I serve the ball high, it is very likely that it will come back high. Similarly, if I serve it low, then most probably it will come back low. That is, our attitudes can influence the behaviour of our partner. It is patience, a quality that is rather rare in our society, that determines the probability of serving and receiving the ball at a height that will enable us to play the game over a long period.

Nowadays we are used to acting impulsively and we expect immediate reactions and responses. For example, we may want to change the way we live but we may fail to realize that we have to change ourselves too and that the process of change itself often involves a long wait. We want the perfect partner and an ideal relationship without perhaps accepting the difficulties this involves.

It should be clear, however, that the only person we can really change is ourself. As we have seen, we can change our outlook on life, our attitudes and what we believe in. We can change what we do and in this way change the situation around us. It is only when we insist on having our own way and stubbornly try to change other people that we court delusion and frustration. If we want others to change, the best thing for us to do is to be generous and let them see the various facets of our personality, leaving them to choose and accept the qualities they prefer.

If we love someone, even what we consider to be their imperfections need not increase the distance between us. We can choose to see these imperfections in a different light and they will not appear to be so bad. It is very important to communicate feelings but this must be done in an open and honest manner and without judging the other person. When a feeling is expressed, it should never be under-valued or ridiculed (perhaps by saying that what the other person sees or feels is insignificant or unreal). Each person's own particular experience is important and real to him.

If we express our thoughts and feelings of joy, we will find it easier to understand one another and lighten the relationship. It is so much nicer to celebrate when there is nothing special or specific to commemorate.

Here is a collection of statements by men and women with a universal message. We would do well to find the courage from time to time to say one or other of these statements out loud, without any false complexes:

- Let me know when you feel lonely or misunderstood. Knowing that I have the power to comfort you will make me feel stronger. Feelings that are not translated into words can become a destructive force. Remember that, even though I love you, I cannot always read your mind.

- Praise me for a job well done and don't belittle me. Rather, reassure me when I make a mess of things. Don't take for granted what I do for you. Appreciation and support will encourage me to carry on.

- Tell me often that you love me using words, gestures and actions. Don't think that I already know it. Maybe I will seem embarrassed and will deny that I need to know this, but don't believe me and do it all the same.

- Let others know you have a good opinion of me. Letting everyone know of our love makes me very proud. We should share with others the feelings of joy that our relationship gives us.

- When you make me feel special, you make up for all those people, who, during the day, pass me by without even noticing me.

I close this chapter with a poem by an anonymous writer who expresses feelings and thoughts that many of us have probably experienced in our attempts to communicate:

When I ask you to listen to me and you start giving me advice,
        you are not doing what I ask you to.
When I ask you to listen to me and you start telling me why I shouldn't feel as I do,
        you are trampling over my feelings.

When I ask you to listen to me and you think you should do
something to solve my problems,

       you disappoint me, strange as it may seem.

Perhaps, this is why prayer works for many.

Because

God is mute. He gives no advice and does not try to put
       things right.

He just listens and trusts you to solve the problems on your
       own.

So I beg you, listen to me and hear me.

And if you want to talk, wait a moment for your turn,

And I promise that I will listen to you . . .

17

Our True Selves

Happiness is an internal state.
It does not depend on what we have
but on what we are.
Henry van Dyke

The Big Questions

What makes you happy? What frightens you? What makes you sad? What do you expect from the future?

The main values and ideals governing our lives depend on the answers we give to certain great questions concerning our existence. Knowing the answers to these questions is very important for a better understanding of ourselves. If we also know the answers our partner would give, this improves communication and the relationship between us in general and can be useful for finding points of commonality or providing opportunities for mutual help and support.

Every question can have many answers. For example, things that make us happy can vary from a good cup of coffee at breakfast time to peace in the world. Our lives are made up of both small and large things. Knowing all these things in detail helps us to be more involved in the happiness of our partner and to be closer to him or her.

Emotions and Feelings

Emotions as such are neither good nor bad. We must convince ourselves that emotions are not moral stances but simple facts. They are part of our nature. Jealousy, anger, sexual desires, fears and so on do not make us either better or worse people. Experts in psychosomatic medicine maintain that today the most frequent cause of tiredness and illness is the repression of emotions.

A great advantage in showing our feelings to our partner is that it encourages him to share his own feelings in a spirit of honesty and openness. That one partner chooses to express his feelings or emotions does not mean, however, that the other partner must also express her feelings, nor should a judgement be made about a partner who does not wish to share her feelings.

It is important to express emotions because otherwise they tend to come out in other ways, to explode like a pressure cooker. Our emotions do not die. They remain alive deep down in our subconscious and they hurt and trouble us. However, we must not always give in to our feelings, whatever the cost. Rather we must recognize and accept them. It is one thing to feel and admit we are afraid and another to allow fear to suffocate us. Similarly, it is one thing to feel and admit we are angry and another to hit someone.

We can, and in fact do, change negative emotional models. We can go from a negative emotion to a more positive one if we recognize and judge it honestly and find it immature and undesirable. We have great powers that we sometimes know nothing about. For example, strange though it may seem, we can choose to be happy or desperately unhappy, masters or slaves, to love or to hate, to forgive or to bear a grudge. This freedom clearly suggests the responsibility we all have in the way we live life. It means that anyone can organize his or her own life at any time and decide to change it.

Our true reality is inside us and is independent of our circumstances. If this were not so, it would be difficult to explain why there is so much unhappiness and frustration among people who live in very positive and indeed enviable material conditions. Hell and heaven are emotional states that we help to build on earth.

Opportunities for Growth

Emotional and psychological suffering weaken us as much as physical pain. Few of us can avoid anxieties or difficulties during our lives. As avoiding difficulties is impossible, we must face them without being overwhelmed by them. One way we might do this is through forgiveness. Forgiveness, in all its forms, is often the only way out of a tunnel of frustration and anxiety. David Augsburger says that forgiveness is letting be what has been, what is and what will be. Through forgiving ourselves and others, we free the self from the past and face the future with greater wisdom, new hope and confidence.

Hope is another fundamental element of our existence. No medicine is so efficient, at some points in our life, as hope. No force gives us more energy than the conviction that every problem has a solution. The power of hope helps us better to face the trials of everyday life. Hope means remembering that we will always find a way out, whatever happens. No one is a hopeless victim and no one should despair, as there are very few situations for which there is truly no resolution and very few ills for which there is no remedy. Through hope we can change a negative situation into a victory. Even if the situation does not change, we can change the way we deal with it. For those who believe, hope is like a gushing fountain of life.

Even in our errors, we can see many opportunities for growth, if we face them as challenges to become more mature. 'Abdu'l-Bahá said: 'The mind and spirit of man advance when he is tried by suffering. The more the ground is ploughed, the better the seed will grow, the better the harvest will be.'[1]

We can summarize under four headings the main forces or powers that motivate people and help us grow:

Decisions

Every human being decides everything, both what he or she feels and what he or she desires. If we admit that all, or nearly all, aspects of our lives are the result of our decisions, we no longer have any excuses for our behaviour. We do not know what will happen to us in the strange mixture of events that is life but we can decide what is happening inside us, how to deal with it and what use to make of it. This is what counts. If we feel lonely, we can do something to get out of that state or at least transform it into an opportunity for productive reflection. If we have a difficult love relationship, we can do something to overcome the problems. We have the power to improve our situation but we must have the will to do so. Solutions to our problems could be close at hand but they do not materialize on their own. They appear only when we genuinely want to find them and decide to take action. As Abraham Lincoln said, 'Most people are as happy as they decide to be.'

The Power of Belief

Perhaps it would be better here to speak of the power of expectation. A well-known example of this power is the case of a workman who was locked in a refrigeration wagon by mistake on a day when it was not in use. The next morning he was found dead from exposure. As the temperature in the wagon was the same as it was outdoors and was not below freezing, there was no explanation for his death. The only possibility that was mooted was that the man was firmly convinced that he would freeze to death.

Every day thousands of people taking placebos actually improve or recover from illness simply because they are convinced of the healing powers of what they are taking. There is a case recorded of a woman who took tablets for years believing them to be contraceptives. She did not become pregnant until a gynaecologist eventually explained that the tablets were not contraceptives but vitamins, whereupon the women almost immediately conceived.

These examples demonstrate that the power of belief can play a significant role in our life. Experience teaches us that life gives us back a little of what we give it. If we believe the world to be unfriendly and we go around with a sullen and suspicious face all the time, for whatever reason, those around us will probably fulfil our expectations – we cannot expect anything particularly comforting to be given to us. If, on the other hand, we face difficulties with optimism and a positive outlook, it is highly probable that we will find ourselves dealing with people who have the same attitude and that the difficulties will easily resolve themselves. Through our expectations we can change the quality of our life.

The Power of Faith

By faith I mean faith in God. If we have a belief in God and have faith that He will help and protect us, we often find that we are more serene in dealing with certain aspects of our life when we draw on this faith. However, our belief must be total and not riddled with doubts. 'Abdu'l-Bahá said that 'Nothing shall be impossible to you if you have faith. As ye have faith so shall your powers and blessings be.'[2] As another sage said, God can mend a broken heart if you give Him all the pieces.

Energy

Each one of us has something, an energy, that is not just physical but psychic – spiritual – and this aspect of our being is the more important of the two. We cannot wait, however, for energy to come before we act, as we will never think we have enough. We must simply act and this will give us new energy. We are like a well of energy: the more we draw from the well, the more we have. This energy is the only thing that never runs out. On the contrary, it feeds itself. It is like certain kinds of plants: the more branches or flowers that are cut off, the more the plant flourishes.

Attributes to Develop

Sometimes we are paralyzed by fear. Fear stems from ignorance, which is the source of all ills. It is important to live life fully, joyfully and spontaneously, to love passionately, without fear, to have high hopes, and never to abandon our dreams, for dreams definitely help us. If we think about it, happiness is simply a complete set of joyous circumstances. We tend to think that happiness is to be found only, or primarily, in comforts and favourable circumstances. However, as Federich Roening pointed out, we forget that happiness cannot be identified with the attainment of something we do not have. Instead, we must identify and appreciate what we already have. 'Abdu'l-Bahá wrote:

> Anybody can be happy in the state of comfort, ease, health, success, pleasure and joy; but if one will be happy

and contented in the time of trouble, hardship and prevailing disease, it is the proof of nobility.[3]

The true development and progress of the individual do not come from the easy things in life but from the attempt to reach goals that seem distant. If we wish to stretch and extend our muscles, when we go to the gym we place the bar high enough so that our hands cannot reach it easily and in this way we are forced to make an effort and stretch. However, this should not become a cause of anxiety or stress, which has now become one of the most common illnesses, or contributors to illness, in our society. Anxiety does not help us change a situation, either in the present or in the future, but it does take away the joy we can derive from little things. We should try to store away in our memories our joyful times so that we can bring them to mind and fall back on them for support when we find ourselves in times of difficulty and there is nothing much to be happy about.

I read the following piece somewhere and I promised myself that this would never happen to me:

> . . . to understand so late and with so much difficulty the useless suffering we endure, or impose on ourselves, and to recall all the opportunities for simple happiness in which I hadn't participated fully, alive and full of warmth, preferring instead to hide behind my mask, a prisoner of my fears, tense in my wild thoughts . . .

Patience is another quality to develop, as it allows us to wait, to understand and to hope. Sometimes it seems as if patience has been completely forgotten in a frenetic world always rushing anxiously to get ahead. Patience generates tranquillity and provides opportunities for meditating on our failures and misapprehensions so that we can use them as means to attain new knowledge and awareness and, thereby, to progress. By being patient, we can solve many of our problems. In our relationship with our partner, the great reward of being patient is lasting love. Anything that is important is worth waiting for with patience.

Finally, we should remember that growth and snares, success and delusion may all be derived from our relationship with our partner, indeed from all relationships. A relationship is positive only when communication is positive. It is only when we are able, in all honesty, to tell ourselves who we are – that is, what we think, feel, love, hope, wish for, respect, believe and what we feel responsible for – that each of us is really able to mature and to have a mature relationship with another person.

Once upon a time, the story goes, a farmer found a little bird in a wood and, believing it to be some kind of chicken, took it back to his farm and put it into the chicken coop with the cock and all the hens. Little by little, the bird grew. One day a hunter who was passing by looked into the chicken coop and saw among the hens a young eagle. He picked it up and took it away with him. He talked to the bird, explaining to it that it wasn't a chicken at all but an eagle. It didn't have to flutter about aimlessly with the hens because it was born to fly over wide open spaces, to soar high and to see far horizons. It was not destined to live in a closed cage. It belonged among the mountains, the valleys and the plains.

We too are eagles and we all have the potential to soar, although we may be the last to suspect it. We must therefore find a way to break out of the cage in which we are enclosed, as we may not be lucky enough to find a hunter to set us free so that we can fly away.

18

Consultation

Learn to listen.
You learn nothing
just listening to yourself.

When we say we know someone, we often use the word 'know' in the same sense that we use it when we say we know something. In other words, knowing another person in this sense means having knowledge that the person exists or knowing something about the person. However, this is rather superficial. Knowing someone really means rediscovering ourselves in that person and, above all, it means being able to share and communicate with him, to open up our hearts, to make ourselves available and to reveal our own thoughts. Instead of always thinking about what we can get out of a relationship, we should think of how we can contribute to it. As long as we have the same goals, it often does not matter that we do not agree with our partner on certain subjects.

When we love a person, it is very important that we keep communication channels open. Communication depends on each partner listening to the other. Listening is an art that has to be learned and developed, just as we must learn to pay due attention to the feelings and peace of mind of others. Humanity has invented fantastic communications systems just to be able to speak to a man on the moon. Yet, often, a mother does not know how to talk with her daughter, a father with his son, a white person with a black, a northerner with a southerner, a husband with his wife.

If we wish truly to communicate with our partner about a problem, we must share our own point of view with him. To do this, we must accept that our partner, too, will have a point of view about the subject and this may well be different from ours. True communication and decision-making require that these points of view be reconciled and this can only be done through consultation. Consultation between a husband and wife is based on rules and principles that must be observed, otherwise what begins as consultation ends in fruitless discussion or even arguments. If the principles of consultation are not observed by both partners, consultation becomes useless and even harmful, as it may be used only to deceive and manipulate the other person.

The Rules of Consultation

• The first rule is to *identify the problem precisely*.

> It may seem strange but often a discussion goes on for hours with each person not only having a different point of view but actually talking about a different problem altogether.

> *She*: You always arrive home late.

> *He*: My job is very stressful and you are always nagging.

• The second rule is to *limit the scope of the problem*.

> Don't raise too many issues and don't bring up problems which, even if they do exist, are not relevant at the

moment. It is better to discuss one problem at a time.

He: The cupboards are always in a mess.

She: You worry more about the cupboards than you do about me.

He: The mess annoys me.

She: You don't love me like you used to.

He: The only thing I want after a stressful day is a bit of peace and quiet.

She: You'll get all the peace you want. I am going out!

And she slams the door behind her.

- The third rule is *never interrupt the other person while he is talking*.

  Even if you think you have understood or, worse, you think the other person is talking a lot of nonsense, listen without prejudice and preconceptions. To listen and to be listened to: this is extremely important. Listening is an active process. We should always remember that each time we listen we can learn something.

  She: What day is it today?

  He: Wednesday.

  She: But what sort of day is it? (i.e. Is it a holiday?)

  He: At the moment it's sunny but it might cloud over soon.

- The fourth rule is *not to reply to an accusation with another accusation.*

  She: Why do you never put your socks in the dirty washing basket?

  He: You're lazy and a spendthrift.

- The fifth rule is to *choose the right time and place for a discussion.*

  Do not try to consult on a problem when the children or strangers are around, or when one of you is pressed for time or is not in a state to face a serious discussion.

  He: Why is it that every time we invite my friend Tony for dinner you burn the roast?

  She: Sorry. I must rush. The kids are late for school.

  He: I knew it! Every time we talk about my friend Tony you rush off. So it's true you don't like him.

- The sixth rule is to *maintain a margin of respect.*

  It is important that each partner show respect to the other, both verbally and in their behaviour.

  She: But have you taken a good look at yourself? And to think I have to stand here listening to a bald, pot-bellied nobody like you!

  He: You worry about your cellulite and let me worry about my belly!

- The seventh rule is to *avoid talking about the past.*

Do not drag up remote episodes from the past to demonstrate that you are right or to support your present arguments.

She: You shouldn't travel by plane. Don't you remember that six years ago a plane was hijacked over Beirut?

He: But it's the same if I go by train. There was a bomb in that tunnel eight years ago.

She: The car is too dangerous. Don't you remember the accident you had three years ago?

He: It's true that I got a flat tyre the last time we went out on our bikes.

She: You see. I'm right when I say that it's better for you to stay at home.

• The eighth rule is to *avoid mentioning the other person's weak points*.

Do not use your partner's weak points, frailties or imperfections as weapons to hurt him. Similarly, you should try to avoid reacting to unkind remarks, egocentrism and childish insults. Such remarks and responses to them simply degrade the relationship and prevent people from getting back together again.

She: What would you know? You were stupid at school and were only able to get your qualifications by going to evening classes.

Him: And what about you? Every time you go out, you have to put on a corset and elastic socks just to hold yourself together. Your whole body is falling apart.

• The ninth rule is to *consider the discussion to be a result of mutual behaviour.*

> Sharing in a love relationship does not mean drawing up a balance sheet of who does this or that, or who does more than the other. There are times when we must give more than we receive but there will be other times when we need to receive more than we are capable of giving. It is impossible to keep score as you might in a sports competition and it is wholly inappropriate to do so in a discussion between two partners whose life together is a joint effort. Keeping an account of our own sufferings makes us victims, while counting our serene moments gives us life.

The Purpose of Consultation

The purpose of consultation is set out in *A Fortress for Well-Being*, a book devoted to the Bahá'í teachings on marriage:

> When tensions or conflicts do arise, they must be identified and discussed, with both frankness and love. For open communication and frequent consultation are essential to the maintenance of unity within a marriage.
>
> Frank consultation is frequently misunderstood to be a process which undermines unity rather than sustains it. Knowledge of possible misunderstanding about the purpose and spirit of consultation and how they can affect the marital relationship may help prevent them or prove useful in dealing with them when they do appear.
>
> 1. Frank consultation is not an aggressive confrontation. Whenever consultation is used as means of expressing hostility, perversity, or rancour, its purpose – which is to find the truth of the situation so action can be taken – is

thwarted. Furthermore, using consultation for giving vent to such negative emotions creates hurt feelings and mistrust which must then be overcome . . .

2. Consultation is not a means for fixing blame, since doing so undermines its basic purpose. Usually, a rehearsal of who did what is unnecessary, since these facts are already known . . . A more important task during consultation is determining the reasons for what caused the difficulty.

3. Consultation is not a forum for nagging . . . Nagging fails to solve the existing problems, and it creates new ones. Nagging robs one of energy and greatly reduces the inclination, on the part of the person who is being nagged, to communicate . . .

4. Consultation should not be used as a substitute for action or a temporary catharsis. Although relief from tension may be one beneficial by-product from consultation, if it does no more than this, it will not foster the growth of the marriage as fully as it might. Consultation should be used to clarify a situation, re-establish the basis of unity, resolve conflicts, and make decisions for action which will help to prevent future difficulties arising from the same issues.

Consultation is not only for problem solving and reaching decisions in regard to difficulties being faced. It is also the means of exchanging and communicating aspirations, lofty ideals, encouragement, and loving support so that the marriage partners may 'improve the spiritual life of each other'. If more time were spent engaging in this kind of consultation, less time would be needed for consultation related to problem solving and the resolution of conflicts.[1]

Problem-Solving

If a problem should arise in our relationship, we must realize that it may have many solutions. In the past we may have felt defeated and discouraged by a problem simply because we did not want to look at it from a different angle – that different angle, of course, was always suggested by another person! Should there be a difference between ourselves and our partner in understanding a problem and its solution, it is very important to put ourselves in the position of our partner. This does not mean that we must totally accept his point of view but simply that we must make an effort to understand it. However, we cannot do this if we do not accept the principle that we are all free to express what we have learned from our own experiences – the lessons another person has learned are always valid for him, even if they contrast with our own findings. We cannot expect everyone to have the same view of life as we do.

When we are consulting with our partner, we must try to achieve a better understanding of his point of view and not to judge him. Consultation is not a time to give our partner advice. As has been said: 'It is better to avoid giving advice: the ignorant take no notice and the wise don't need it.'

If sometimes in consultation we find we have to give way to our partner, this does not mean we have 'surrendered' or that he has 'won', just as being flexible does not mean we are unprincipled. Such an attitude is not in the spirit of consultation, which attempts to achieve consensus and unity. In any case, it often happens that by giving up something we receive much more than we expected in return. There is a Persian proverb that says: 'With courtesy and kind words you can lead an elephant by a hair.' Similarly, Dean Rusk said: 'Our own ears are one of the best tools we have for convincing other people . . . by listening to what they have to say.'

19

Conclusion

I have now reached the end of what seems to me to be more like a long letter than a book, a letter written to dear friends in which I have tried to express my thoughts and, above all, my feelings. I do not want to conclude with my own inadequate words but rather with those of 'Abdu'l-Bahá who gave this advice to a man contemplating marriage and whose words of wisdom have a universal application:

> The bond that unites hearts most perfectly is loyalty. True lovers once united must show forth the utmost faithfulness one to an other. You must dedicate your knowledge, your talents, your fortunes, your titles, your bodies and your spirits to God, to Bahá'u'lláh and to each other. Let your hearts be spacious, as spacious as the universe of God!
>
> Allow no trace of jealousy to creep between you, for jealousy, like unto poison, vitiates the very essence of love. Let not the ephemeral incidents and accidents of this changeful life cause a rift between you. When differences present themselves, take counsel together in secret, lest others magnify a speck into a mountain. Harbour not in your hearts any grievance, but rather explain its nature to each other with such frankness and understanding that it will disappear, leaving no remembrance. Choose fellowship and amity and turn away from jealousy and hypocrisy.

Your thoughts must be lofty, your ideals luminous, your minds spiritual, so that you souls may become a dawning-place for the Sun of Reality. Let your hearts be like two pure mirrors reflecting the stars of the heaven of love and beauty.

Together make mention of noble aspirations and heavenly concepts. Let there be no secrets one from another. Make your house a haven of rest and peace. Be hospitable, and let the doors of your house be open to the faces of friends and strangers. Welcome every guest with radiant grace and let each feel that it is his own home.

No mortal can conceive the union and harmony which God has designed for man and wife. Nourish continually the tree of your union with love and affection, so that it will remain ever green and verdant throughout all seasons and bring forth luscious fruits for the healing of nations.

O beloved of God, may your home be a vision of the paradise of Abhá, so that whosoever enters there may feel the essence of purity and harmony, and cry out from the heart: 'Here is the home of love! Here is the palace of love! Here is the nest of love! Here is the garden of love!'

Be like two sweet-singing birds perched upon the highest branches of the tree of life, filling the air with songs of love and rapture.

Lay the foundation of your affection in the very centre of your spiritual being, at the very heart of your consciousness, and let it not be shaken by adverse winds.

And when God gives you sweet and lovely children, consecrate yourselves to their instruction and guidance, so that they may become imperishable flowers of the divine rose-garden, nightingales of the ideal paradise, servants of the world of humanity, and the fruit of the tree of your life.

Live in such harmony that others may take your lives for an example and may say one to another: 'Look how they live like two doves in one nest, in perfect love, affinity and union. It is as though from all eternity God had kneaded the very essence of their beings for the love of one another.'

Attain the ideal love that God has destined for you, so that you may become partakers of eternal life forthwith. Quaff deeply from the fountain of truth, and dwell all the days of your life in a paradise of glory, gathering immortal flowers from the garden of divine mysteries.

Be to each other as heavenly lovers and divine beloved ones dwelling in a paradise of love. Build your nest on the leafy branches of the tree of love. Soar into the clear atmosphere of love. Sail upon the shoreless sea of love. Walk in the eternal rose-garden of love. Bathe in the shining rays of the sun of love. Be firm and steadfast in the path of love. Perfume your nostrils with the fragrance from the flowers of love. Attune your ears to the soul-entrancing melodies of love. Let your aims be as generous as the banquets of love, and your words as a string of white pearls from the ocean of love. Drink deeply of the elixir of love, so that you may live continually in the reality of Divine Love.[1]

Bibliography

'Abdu'l-Bahá. *Paris Talks*. London: Bahá'í Publishing Trust, 1967.

—— *Selections from the Writings of 'Abdu'l-Bahá*. Haifa: Bahá'í World Centre, 1978.

Bahá'í Prayers: A Selections of Prayers revealed by Bahá'u'lláh, the Báb and 'Abdu'l-Bahá. Wilmette, Ill.: Bahá'í Publishing Trust, 1991.

Bahá'í Prayers for Special Occasions. London: Bahá'í Publishing Trust, 1954.

Bahá'í World Faith. Wilmette, Ill.: Bahá'í Publishing Trust, 2nd edn. 1976.

Bahá'u'lláh. *Gleanings from the Writings of Bahá'u'lláh*. Wilmette, Ill.: Bahá'í Publishing Trust, 1983.

—— *The Hidden Words*. Wilmette, Ill.: Bahá'í Publishing Trust, 1990.

—— *Kitáb-i-Íqán*. Wilmette, Ill.: Bahá'í Publishing Trust, 1989.

—— *The Seven Valleys and the Four Valleys*. Wilmette, Ill.: Bahá'í Publishing Trust, 1991.

Bahíyyih Khánum, the Greatest Holy Leaf: A Compilation from Bahá'í Sacred Texts and Writings of the Guardian of the Faith and Bahíyyih Khánum's Own Letters. Haifa: Bahá'í World Centre, 1982.

Blumenthal, Erik. *The Way to Inner Freedom*. Oxford: Oneworld, 1988.

Compilation of Compilations, The. Prepared by the Universal House of Justice 1963-1990. 2 vols. [Sydney]: Bahá'í Publications Australia, 1991.

A Fortress for Well-Being: Bahá'í Teachings on Marriage. Wilmette, Ill.: Bahá'í Publishing Trust, 1973.

Fromm, Erich. *The Art of Loving*. London: Thorsons, 1995.

Gibran, Kahlil. *The Prophet*. Harmondsworth, Middx: Arkana, Penguin Books, 1992.

Tannen, Deborah. *That's Not What I Meant! How Conversational Style Makes or Breaks Relationships*. New York: Ballentine Books, 1986.

—— *You Just Don't Understand: Women and Men in Conversation*. London: Virago Press, 1992.

References

Preface

1. This was said by Don Abbondio, a character in the novel *The Betrothed* by the 19th-century Italian writer Alessandro Manzoni. Don Abbondio was a parish priest who, although well-intentioned, caused the betrothed couple a lot of trouble through his own lack of courage.

Chapter 1: Never Take a Relationship for Granted

1. Bahá'u'lláh, *Seven Valleys*.

Chapter 2: Regular Servicing

1. 'Abdu'l-Bahá, *Selections*, p. 118.
2. Attributed to 'Abdu'l-Bahá, in *Bahá'í Prayers for Special Occasions*, p. 47.

Chapter 4: Openness and Frankness

1. Bahá'u'lláh, *Gleanings*, pp. 4-5.
2. 'Abdu'l-Bahá, *Selections*, p. 118.
3. Attributed to 'Abdu'l-Bahá, in *Bahá'í Prayers for Special Occasions*, p. 47.
4. Bahá'u'lláh, *Kitáb-i-Íqán*, p. 193.

Chapter 5: Respect

1. Bahá'u'lláh, *Hidden Words*, Arabic no. 30.
2. 'Abdu'l-Bahá, *Paris Talks*, p. 174.
3. Bahá'u'lláh, *Hidden Words*, Arabic no. 3.

4. Bahá'u'lláh, *Hidden Words*, Arabic no. 13.
5. Attributed to 'Abdu'l-Bahá, in *Bahá'í Prayers for Special Occasions*, p. 47.

Chapter 6: Mature Love

1. Fromm, *Art of Loving*, p. 32.
2. From a letter written on behalf of Shoghi Effendi to an individual believer, 12 May 1925, in *Compilation*, pp. 3–4.
3. Gibran, *The Prophet*, pp. 18–21.

Chapter 8: Special Moments Together

1. Advice of Mrs Margaret Ruhe, given in 1971.

Chapter 9: Developing Goals, Realizing Potential

1. Bahá'u'lláh, *Bahá'í Prayers*, p. 105.
2. Bahá'u'lláh, *Gleanings*, p. 261.
3. 'Regard man as a mine rich in gems of inestimable value. Education can, alone, cause it to reveal its treasures, and enable mankind to benefit therefrom.' Bahá'u'lláh, *Gleanings*, p. 260.

Chapter 10: The Spiritual Bond

1. Attributed to 'Abdu'l-Bahá, in *Bahá'í Prayers for Special Occasions*, p. 48.
2. ibid.

Chapter 11: Interchangeable and Flexible Roles

1. From a letter written on behalf of Shoghi Effendi to an individual believer, 16 March 1949, in *Compilation*, vol. 2, pp. 19–20.

Chapter 14: Thinking Positively

1. Fromm, *Art of Loving*, p. 39.
2. Quoted in Blumenthal, *Way to Inner Freedom*, p. 109.

Chapter 16: Communication

1. See Tannen, *You Just Don't Understand* and *That's Not What I Meant!*

Chapter 17: Our True Selves

1. 'Abdu'l-Bahá, *Paris Talks*, p. 178.
2. 'Abdu'l-Bahá, cited by Bahíyyih Khánum in *Bahíyyih Khánum*, p. 225.
3. 'Abdu'l-Bahá, in *Bahá'í World Faith*, p. 363.

Chapter 18: Consultation

1. *Fortress for Well-Being*, pp. 68–70.

Chapter 19: Conclusion

1. Attributed to 'Abdu'l-Bahá, in *Bahá'í Prayers for Special Occasions*, pp. 47–50.